# Prayers for Parishes

Rupert Bristow

kevin
mayhew

*For Sarah, Michael and Richard*

kevin mayhew

First published in 2011 by Kevin Mayhew Ltd.
Buxhall, Stowmarket, Suffolk IP14 3BW
Tel: +44 (0) 1449 737978 Fax: +44 (0) 1449 737834
E-mail: info@kevinmayhewltd.com

www.kevinmayhew.com



ISBN 978 1 84867 338 0
Catalogue No. 1501256

Cover design by Rob Mortonson
© Image used under licence from Shutterstock Inc.
Edited by Rebecca Henning
Typeset by Rob Mortonson

Printed and bound in Great Britain

# Contents

# About the author

Rupert Bristow was Director of Education for Canterbury Diocese from 1995 until his retirement in 2008 and is active as a Reader in Trinity Benefice, Folkestone. He has chaired Kent SACRE (Standing Advisory Council for Religious Education) and has worked in education – in schools, universities and administration – at home and overseas. Rupert has edited and written for various educational publications. He is an Honorary Fellow of Canterbury Christ Church University.

## Other books by Rupert Bristow

*Prayers for Education (2005)*

*Only Connect (2009)*

*Sunday Intercessions (2010)*

# Foreword

*Prayers for Parishes,* though written primarily for Anglican use, is a book which will appeal to Christians of all traditions.

The language of worship, the emphases in worship, the styles of worship – all have changed from what they were 20 or 30 years ago and, added to this, the issues which need to be prayed about have developed and changed as society and the world have changed. This book, in its contemporary approach and style, seeks to meet these needs and to do so not from any one, narrow, theological position, but from a perspective that recognises the comprehensive nature of the Christian Church. What is said in public worship always needs to unite and not divide those who are being led in their approach to God. For this reason, the very careful choice of words, which characterises these prayers, is essential in public worship.

It would be a mistake to assume that the prayers in this book are suitable only for use in public: they can give an added dimension to private worship, and they are suitable for family worship as well as small group worship. However, the fact that the majority of the prayers are intercessory makes them an invaluable resource for the many, in all churches, who hold the responsibility of leading eucharistic intercessions. The way in which these prayers are constructed easily allows a phrase, a line, a petition to be culled, so as to give depth, substance and thrust to that section of the Eucharist which is so difficult to lead inspirationally. Used in this way, the book supplements previous books by Rupert Bristow.

This book is needed and I warmly commend it.

**John A. Simpson**
*Dean-Emeritus of Canterbury*

# Introduction

**This book**

This book of prayers has taken shape over a year or so, partly as a response to a love of books of prayers produced 20 or 30 years ago which I have found to be a constant source of refreshment and reference. Among these were the prayers of Frank Colquhoun, who never failed to provide, through his writings or judicious choice of the work of others, prayers fit for and appropriate to many parish situations and world events. His were the books to go to for inspiration and a deft and relevant touch. They were appreciated and used in churches and in private prayer. And he was a master of the English language.

My aim here has not been to try to 'update' Frank Colquhoun's magnificent and still moving prayers, but to attempt my own style of prayers for different situations and different purposes that might be encountered in the parishes of today and tomorrow. My prayers are written to encourage and challenge rather than to replace the authentic voice of the person praying. Indeed, I rather hope that in some cases the reader's reaction will be to decide to use very different words; but at least I may have given food for thought in formulating a more personally relevant prayer appropriate to the context.

I have deliberately offered a variety of prayers under each heading, to enable people to choose the one that most closely accords with the context. Most are appropriate both for formal situations, such as intercessions in church, and for more personal, private prayer, as well as in a group. I hope they will complement and supplement my book offering sets of prayers following the Lectionary, *Sunday Intercessions.* This could be a useful book to have in the church vestry or as a companion for study or bedroom. I hope you enjoy using it – and reacting to it.

**Why pray?**

First, our Lord wants us to pray! If that is not enough (and it should be), prayers have formed a continuous thread over time and across the world. They have been expressions of faith and entreaties to God over the ages and across cultures. In many ways they are the bedrock of our personal relationship with God, through Jesus Christ. Music may give our prayers wings, readings from the Bible may give knowledge and understanding, sermons may interpret; but, in the end, our connection with our Lord is given meaning and substance through our prayers, silent or said, private or communal, extemporary or read.

We may pray more when things are going wrong than when things are going well, but, if we develop a pattern of prayer, daily or morning and evening, we can more easily share the good and the bad with a God who knows and cares for us as whole people. Our prayer can be pleading for something to happen (or not happen), thanking God for what has happened and interceding for others, loved ones or people in various kinds of need.

Prayers that are available in book form or from the internet may fill a need when we are unable to find the right words – or when we simply feel tongue-tied. Books still have the edge in terms of leafing through likely topics or headings, I think!

Of course the prayer our Lord taught us is still the well-spring and inspiration for all our prayers, and is the one turned to first and last in any situation. Its depth and simplicity are unsurpassed. What we want out of prayer, I suggest, is an experience that articulates inner needs and feelings which we want to share with God. What he then does with them is not for us to demand or know, but our persistence in prayer is a duty and a privilege and in itself therapeutic. It establishes and maintains a relationship which needs the practice of prayer to feed and nurture it.

## Where and when to pray

There is no right place or time to pray, so people often find unusual settings for their regular prayer, from time in the car or on the train to dog-walking or preparing breakfast. And it's still OK to get down on your knees, though a comfy chair has its advantages – especially for periods of silent reflection. But a quick prayer before an important meeting, saying grace before a meal or a prayer of thanks after an ordeal overcome or before a difficult pastoral situation not encountered before – all of these often in the form of short 'arrow' prayers – are all valid and entirely appropriate, it seems to me!

Then of course there is church, where prayer is both an important ingredient of any service and a place where people go to be quiet before God, often in times of trouble or great need. Churches need to make it possible and easy for this to happen – and not just for regular churchgoers. One or two ideas on how to make this a user-friendly experience are given at the end of this book, together with some sample prayers of the kind you might like to have available in your church as a customised complement or supplement to this book – and to take away if necessary.

Of course the 'when and where of prayer' also has an implicit sequential element. Prayer may precede, go alongside or come after whatever we are praying about. Put another way, the prayer could be a starter or a dessert, but sometimes it can be the main course, the main event. We should never underestimate the power, depth and experience of a 'prayer day' or a 'prayer vigil' or a silent retreat; a subject I return to under the section on Resources at the end of the book.

## How to pray

Over the centuries and across different denominations there has been a huge variety of forms and approaches to prayer. One of the major differences concerns the question of to whom the prayer is addressed: Father/God; Son/Jesus; Holy Spirit; Mary; other saints? In this book and in many Anglican traditions the usual practice has been to address God directly, seeking intercession through Jesus, but in some traditions Mary features heavily as the one through whom prayers are directed; yet others seek to address Jesus directly. This is not the place to say what is doctrinally correct, and it seems entirely valid to invoke or enlist saintly figures as back-up to our prayers; but surely we all seek to have a direct relationship, especially in prayer, with God, who is indeed Father, Son and Holy Spirit as we believe, but who is still, first and last, Almighty God.

The language we use to pray seems a relevant issue only insofar as it should be a language and a style which we find comfortable to use. And if we do, we should have confidence that God does too! If an old prayer we have found seems to express what we want to share with God and it happens to contain the occasional 'Thee' or 'Thou', so be it! We can use that language or change it to fit the purpose.

**Listening to God**

Prayer is a two-way process. Think of a conversation with someone who doesn't allow you to get a word in edgeways. How do you feel? Of course there are times when a good counsellor hardly says anything, just listens. And God is, as we know, a 'Mighty Counsellor'. But if we really want to learn from our discussion with God, then shouldn't we allow some quality 'listening time' ourselves? Silent prayer can cover a multitude of sins, but it should allow true silence, in the midst of our rage or pleadings or thanksgiving, in order to see the mind of God, or at least allow him to work on our thoughts and feelings in order to restore, reconcile or acknowledge our praise and thanks.

Listening to God has been a feature of our faith from biblical times and, in the midst of our busyness today, it is still a bulwark of our lives as Christians who really want to know and serve God.

**Is prayer answered?**

Of course there is our time, then there is God's time. Miraculous responses to prayer, especially in the area of healing and wholeness, are almost commonplace. But for most of us, most of the time, the answer to our prayers is more diffuse than that. To feel that God is listening is in itself a response. To know for certain that he has responded in a particular way is more difficult to ascertain. But the number of times apparent coincidences have seemed to be 'God-incidences' is legion. And God's answer to our prayers rarely seems to be at the time or in the manner of our choosing. But that is the wonder and the mystery of our living faith, not a matter of God failing to co-operate with our wishes. We must all work out our own expectations and our response to what, if anything, emerges. And what actually happens may often prove to be far in advance of what we prayed for in the first place.

Keep praying . . .

# The Church

# National Church

Heavenly Father,
give to your Church the faith and the firmness
to weather the storms of controversy,
by discerning your purpose for the people of God,
by sharing your word through ministry and mission
and by sharing your love with those of faith
and with those with none.
Pour down on your bishops and priests
the stamina and the inspiration
to maintain and sustain your presence in the world,
through the grace that you have shown
through your Son.
Amen.

Lord God,
you have shown us through your Son
and in the work of the disciples,
the saints and your pilgrim people,
that your Church is a force in the world.
Let all your people know
that the responsibility is ours
to minister and to pray,
to bring wholeness and caring,
to lighten the burdens of others.
May the pastoral witness of the churches
snuff out the taunts and jibes
of those who see only structures
instead of Christ at work.
Shine the light of hope and the beacon of faith in the world,
empowering God.
Amen.

Almighty God,
we pray for our Church leaders,
our archbishops and bishops,
and all who influence the future of the Church,
including those on Archbishops' Council and General Synod,
and those who serve on Bishops' Advisory Panels.
Create in them the capacity to grasp and resolve issues
and to discern your will in all they do.
May relationships between denominations and between faiths
be blessed with respect and affection
at both national and local levels,
to give reconciliation the best hope of success.
Amen.

Lord and Father,
bless our Church and its leaders;
bless our priests and laity;
bless our buildings and communities.
In return, may we give our best efforts
to the development of your Church,
in maturity and in response to the world,
so that our personal prayers and preoccupations
can be given wider vision and clearer focus.
Stretch us, Lord, inside out,
upside down, every which way,
so that we can be tested
– and not found wanting, we pray.
Amen.

# Local Church

Lord God,
we give thanks for our church
and this your congregation.
Bring us insight and inspiration
so that we can know your presence
and worship your majesty.
But help us also to reach out to our neighbouring churches,
learning from them and listening to them,
showing and sharing their fellowship
and joining together on mission projects
in our community and beyond.
May our focus be local
but our vision much wider,
as your Son's was.
Amen.

Almighty God,
make us, your people, your true servants,
not only in church but also in community.
May we welcome people in
and may they feel your Holy Spirit in this place.
Give to those who minister here
and all who worship your name
the confidence to pray in hope
and the means to do your will.
Let us be a church which loves you
and a church where you are teaching us
to be more like your Son,
our Saviour, Jesus Christ.
Amen.

God of beauty and might,
look down on our worshipping community,
and on our church, with grace and with mercy.
Heal us when we suffer.
Challenge us when we are content.
Bring us to an understanding of our neighbours
as we understand more about you.
And may we see Jesus
in all that we attempt here,
in our worship and praise
and in our mission and ministry.
May we always feel your presence
– and rejoice.
Amen.

Lord of great things and small things,
you know the value of each person
and make us all feel special.
May every church make a difference,
every prayer matter,
and every kindness show your love.
Let our church be a place
where all are welcome,
visitor, stranger, young, old,
and where you are present
in all our actions and activities,
in our busyness and in your peace.
Help us to look forwards and look up,
even when we are deeply in prayer,
for your Son's sake.
Amen.

# Clergy and laity

Great Shepherd of the sheep,
show your pastoral care to your flock,
priests and readers, ordained and lay,
office-holders and congregation members.
May we all contribute our gifts and insights,
showing obedience to your will,
whatever our role and position.
May we think collectively and act individually
in accordance with your vision for the Church
your Son would wish to see.
Amen.

Father of all,
pour down your Holy Spirit
on bishops, priests, deacons and lay ministers;
your gifts of preaching and prophecy,
healing and pastoral care.
And may we all be receptive
to your holy word and sacrament,
in our worship and devotions,
so that in our daily lives
we can be your disciples and missioners,
witnessing to your grace,
showing your hospitality
and reflecting your love,
with the help of your Son, our Saviour, Jesus Christ.
Amen.

God of order and justice,
bring to your clergy and laity
an openness to your will
and a responsibility to each other,
so that together we can be your Church, not just ours.
May we honour authority
wherever it is exercised in your name,
and may we act responsibly in our various roles,
so that we properly honour you
and serve your purpose.
As we seek to carry out your mission to us,
may we do justice to the sacrifices of the disciples
and your Son, Jesus Christ.
Amen.

Holy Lord,
grant to your bishops, priests and deacons
a share of your transforming love,
and to laity a partnership
of discipleship and sharing.
Shape our vision to yours
and direct our energies to the tasks
you help us to identify.
Give us courage in our endeavours
and patience in our perseverance.
And give us the insight to follow your ways
in holiness and peace, all our days.
Amen.

# The world Church

Almighty God,
we ask for your blessings on the worldwide Church.
Wherever your name is known and honoured,
let righteousness and justice flourish.
Where your Church is persecuted,
give courage and comfort to those affected
and bring renewal and relief.
May Church leaders of every denomination
respect each other as they worship you.
And may congregations in different countries
grow in their knowledge and understanding of diversity.
We are one body because we share one bread.
Amen.

Gracious Lord,
bring inspiration and encouragement to your Church.
Over centuries you have made your purpose known
through men and women of faith,
saints and martyrs, clergy and laity.
Give to us today that same spark of the Holy Spirit,
so that we can do you justice,
not just in our churches,
but in our witness to others
and our support and prayers
for churches across the world.
May we lift high the cross
as a duty and a privilege.
Amen.

Creator God,
you are Lord of the universe.
Let those who worship you
be strengthened in the Spirit,
be tested and not found wanting,
be good neighbours and strong witnesses.
Above all, may all who profess your name
know your love and receive your forgiveness.
Let the spirit of truth
break down the barriers of hate
so that all may be free.
Amen.

God of fellowship,
may church communities flourish throughout the world
whatever the circumstances around them.
May you grow disciples where they are needed
and sustain faith
where two or three are gathered together in your name.
Let worship take many forms,
but always with your Son as its focus,
you as our plumb line,
and the Holy Spirit as our guide.
Inspire every nation
to hear your word and know your love,
with the help of your Son, Jesus Christ.
Amen.

# Ecumenical

Lord of all,
let the fellowship of all believers
break through suspicions of different traditions.
Give to each denomination the will and the means
to confer together, work together
and subsume their distinctiveness
in the great mission of extending your kingdom.
May churches together
be greater than the sum of their parts,
for the sake of your Son, Jesus Christ.
Amen.

Universal God, Heavenly Father,
you give to your people the freedom
to choose or reject you.
You have also seen your Church
divide and merge, struggle and unite.
In all this, may humankind's influence
be put aside in church matters,
so that denominations can see
what is common to us all
and how little we differ
in love for you,
in love of neighbour,
in response to need,
and in advancing your kingdom.
Amen.

Almighty God,
who wants the best for us,
help us to give our best to you,
not just in worship
but in our daily round.
And let us join together
on the feast days and great festivals
to join our voices and forces
in praise of you,
as we seek a glimpse of you
in your great mission to us,
your Son, Jesus Christ.
Amen.

God of harmony and purpose,
may we come to grow in ecumenical co-operation
in our community,
in our land,
and across the worldwide Church.
Your Son showed us the right path,
yet we have strayed down blind alleys,
as well as highways and byways,
ostensibly in search of you,
but often to meet our own goals.
Create in us, we pray,
the compass we need
to have a right relationship with you,
forgiving and patient Lord.
Amen.

# Church unity

In the power of the Spirit and in union with Christ,
we pray for the unity of your Church.
You inspired the disciples to build up the Church you created
and it is our discipleship which must sustain it.
Whatever divisions have grown up between denominations,
never let us take our eyes off your Son,
never let us forget what our churches are for,
and never let us stray from your purpose;
but may we always seek partnership and reconciliation,
as your Son did.
Amen.

Great God,
you are bigger than our imagination can comprehend.
May we rise above the limitations
of structures that seek to confine you.
But may our patterns of worship
celebrate your generosity
and the abundance of your creation,
in the variety, quality and reflectiveness of the liturgy,
so that young and old, rich and poor,
newcomers and long-standing members
can join in celebrating and praising you,
our Father, Son and Holy Spirit.
Amen.

Father of all,
you bring all things together
through your Son and Holy Spirit.
Give to us a true insight into your ways,
so that the different churches can reflect
that central unity in their diversity.
May tough decisions and major differences
be tackled in the spirit of sacrifice
and the love of self and neighbour
that your Son showed us.
Then all things will be made new,
in the light of Christ.
Amen.

Almighty God,
you created us in your image,
but in our rebellion we let you down.
In the restored relationship your Son gave us,
through his incarnation, crucifixion and resurrection,
we were given a second chance.
We pray that in sustaining your Church
in all its various forms
we may find a way to unity,
working alongside each other
in partnership, collaboration and sometimes healthy tension.
Give us the vision to see beyond our differences
and into the unity of your purpose.
Amen.

# Church in society

Merciful Father,
help us as Christians to play our full part
in our society and community,
both as individuals and as a church.
Your Son taught us not to set ourselves apart,
but to treat neighbour as self,
not to seek position or look down on others,
and to seek you in the poor and outcast.
Let the mission of our churches reflect these priorities,
engaging with society
and taking a prophetic role where necessary,
as witnesses to your will for us.
Amen.

Caring Lord,
may we take our social responsibility seriously,
as Christians, as citizens, as your disciples.
Give us the desire and capacity
to serve you in serving others;
to challenge those who ignore the public good;
to champion the marginalised, the deprived, the oppressed;
and to share your hope in the love of Christ.
May your kingdom embrace our big society
with the inspiration of the Holy Spirit.
Amen.

Heavenly Father,
pour down your blessings on the structures of our society.
May they work for those they serve,
not for the status or power of those in charge.
Help your Church to be an example and model,
working collaboratively and selflessly,
reaching out as your Son showed us,
empowering others to take responsibility
as your Son did,
and using the judgement and creativity
you have given us
to make a difference in your world.
Amen.

Almighty God,
bring us better understanding and insight
as we seek transformation in society.
May our efforts prosper
if they are grounded in prayer, research and reflection.
Help us to take the necessary steps
to equip ourselves for the tasks ahead,
learning from others,
praying for courage and confidence,
and taking risks for you,
knowing that you will pick us up
as long as we have failed in good faith
rather than backed away in fear.
May we always ask what your Son would have done,
as the Church responds to problems in society.
Amen.

# Relationship to other faiths

God of power and might,
bless all who confess their faith
through revelation, upbringing, culture or teaching.
We count our blessings as Christians
that you have shown us the way,
the truth and the light
through your Son's incarnation
and our salvation through the cross.
May those of other faiths respect ours
and may we as Christians
show hospitality and generosity
in our relationship with them.
Give us broad shoulders
and faithful hearts.
Amen.

Immanent God,
let all the nations know your name
and may all peoples feel your love.
Give to people of all faiths and none
the opportunity to turn to you,
helped by our witness, our openness
and our respect for neighbour and friend,
stranger and traveller.
May we seek to understand those of different faiths,
as every person is precious in your eyes.
We ask for the insight of your Holy Spirit
so that we can relate to all your creation.
Amen.

God of difference and inclusion,
your Son related to Jew and Gentile,
to sinner and Samaritan,
to publican and prostitute,
to tax collector and outcast.
May we be as inclusive and open,
not only to individuals
but also to other faiths,
even when we are the object of antagonism.
Help us to be open to learn through exposure to challenge,
and may we be inspired
by the saints and martyrs down the ages,
with the help of your Son, Jesus Christ.
Amen.

Loving Lord,
you are forever young –
and timeless too.
Have mercy on all in this life
as we come and go.
May the love that you have for us
be felt by all who turn to you.
Help us to witness to that love in our own lives
so that, by your grace,
people of other faiths may be drawn to you
and our differences be seen in perspective,
God of time and space.
Amen.

# Fresh expressions

God of old and new,
bring to our worship and praise
a freshness and authenticity
that leads us straight to you.
May we look to new contexts
and draw on our experience of your creation
to make church relevant,
to draw people in to worship
and to reach out to those
who have never called on you.
Give us the inspiration and confidence
to follow your disciples' footsteps
and engage with people
where they are – and where you are too.
Amen.

God of the new,
bring us joy in worship;
make our music emotional;
give us the gift of meaningful prayer.
Let café, school and pub
be your church where that seems right.
But also let the inherited church
burst forth in fresh expressions,
bringing joy and revelation
to young and old, churched and unchurched,
joined together in praising you.
Amen.

Lord God,
bringer of good news,
through your Son, amaze us!
Help us to think what he might like
if he were in our midst today.
Where would he expect us to worship?
Where would he proclaim your word?
And where would he find you?
In the ordinary and the extraordinary,
let us prepare and be prepared
to worship you in full voice
and with open hearts.
Amen.

Creative Lord,
send down on us the inspiration for renewal
in our praise and in our hearts.
Let our liturgy breathe with new life
in sacred places and in different settings.
Your Son showed us your way,
your truth and your life.
Help us to update our image of you,
to do justice to the vision
of Father, Son and Holy Spirit
left by your Son's disciples,
the cornerstone of our faith,
yesterday, today and tomorrow.
Amen.

# At parochial church councils

Almighty God,
be with us in our deliberations
as we seek to discern your will
for our church and congregation.
May we listen more than speak,
reflect before we decide,
and always consider how our decisions
may advance your kingdom.
Give us insight and wisdom
and the commitment to see things through.
Amen.

Heavenly Father,
bring to our meeting clarity and purpose,
the willingness to do things properly,
but also to take risks for you.
Fill our discussions with your Holy Spirit,
so that we keep to your grand design
and make decisions which shape our mission
and reflect your will.
And may we be good listeners,
to each other and to you;
we ask in Jesus' name.
Amen.

Father of all,
we ask for your presence with us now
in our deliberations and debate.
May we disagree in love
and compromise with generosity,
always drawing on the principles
your Son shared with us.
So help us to foresee the impact of our decisions
on the poor and the weak
as well as the rich and strong;
on the visitor and stranger
as well as the regular attender.
Give us insight and judgement, we pray,
as we begin our meeting.
Amen.

Lord God,
help us as we meet to focus on what you would want of us.
Make this a time for prayer in action,
working your purpose out together, in fellowship.
Bring us a sense of responsibility to others and to you;
bring us a sense of excitement as we confer about the future;
bring us a sense of what has gone before,
so that we can build on firm foundations
of faith, of service, of love.
Amen.

# At synods

Almighty God,
grant to your synod wisdom in our proceedings,
a desire to extend your kingdom,
and the ability to choose the right priorities.
We value the gift of debate
and honour the right to disagree.
But may all that we do
be according to your will
for the good of your Church.
Amen.

God of hope,
may the issues before us at this synod
be viewed through the prism of Christian love.
Let us voice and examine every concern
as we seek to discern the best ways forward.
Give us the courage to challenge,
and if necessary change, our structures
in order that we may show
that your kingdom comes first
in our procedures as in our lives.
Amen.

Lord God,
you have given us the freedom to choose.
May there be freedom of debate today
within the bounds of respect and propriety.
May we seek to shape policy and practice
to meet the needs of both maintenance and mission,
using the precious gift of finance
to support and extend the ministry of your Church
in a world of spiritual deprivation and need.
Amen.

Father of all,
as your Church seeks to withstand the forces of secularism,
may we feel empowered and emboldened,
by your Holy Spirit, to implement your agenda
rather than respond to the agenda of others.
Strengthen our vision for the future of our diocese *(deanery)*
and bring forward people of quality to do your work
in our parishes and deaneries,
in our churches and communities,
with the help of your Son, Jesus Christ.
Amen.

# Pilgrimage

God of place and purpose,
we give thanks for the saints who have gone before
and whose lives have inspired our pilgrimage.
As we seek out the clues of their legacy,
may we see Jesus in their actions,
may we see you in their judgement,
may we see the Holy Spirit in their faith.
Amen.

God of movement,
as we travel through lands and places
that are new to us – but not to you –
may we take care to get to know the people too,
so that we may better understand
the saints who lived and worked there.
Help us to know their relationship with you, Lord,
and teach us how we can learn from them
in restoring our own faith connections
with ourselves, our neighbours and, above all,
with your Son, our Saviour, Jesus Christ.
Amen.

God of the new creation,
unfold for us on our journey
how these saints helped
to keep faith alive,
to reveal truth,
to witness to others
and to make a difference in the world.
May we in our small way
recreate that sense of purpose and mission
not just on our journey
but in our hearts and in our lives,
so that on our return
we can refresh and be refreshed,
renew and be renewed.
Amen.

Almighty God,
we are a pilgrim people
and you are a constant star
who brings us to the next place in safety.
Guide us on our journey
so that we know when to stop and wonder
and when to press on to the next place.
As you led your people out of the wilderness,
as you inspired your disciples to go out and do your work,
and as you watch over us in our travels to new places,
sustain us spiritually and physically
for the tasks as well as the spectacles ahead of us.
Amen.

# Discipleship

Father of all,
you did not count the cost when you sent your Son to be with us.
Strengthen us in our discipleship;
steel us in our endeavour;
carry us in our struggle.
Help us to face up to our responsibilities
in being faithful and true,
not only in our own faith,
but in sharing the good news.
At work, at home, in our community,
may we stand up for you,
remembering your Son was cut down for us.
Amen.

Loving Lord,
help us to follow the tough love of your Son
in all our dealings in the world.
May we put our relationship with your Son
before all else, knowing that,
in doing so, we may grow closer to each other,
joining together in faith,
listening together in love,
armed with your Holy Spirit,
in union with you and your Son,
resisting evil and restoring trust.
Amen.

God of mercy,
whose amazing grace empowers us to follow your Son's ways,
set out your requirements of us,
however difficult they may be.
We know that, through your Church,
and with the help of your Holy Spirit,
we can rise to the challenges we face.
May we be inspired by your disciples,
those who built on the foundations of your Church,
those who kept the flame of faith alive
and those who serve you now,
through your Son, our Saviour, Jesus Christ.
Amen.

Comforter, Counsellor, King of kings,
we pray for your wise counsel
alongside your judgement and justice,
as we seek to be good disciples.
May we see the challenge of discipleship
as an honour and an opportunity,
even though at times it will be difficult.
Give to your Church and our parish
the wisdom and empathy
to support our tentative efforts,
not necessarily openly and publicly,
but through prayer and pastoral sensitivity.
Give us hope that we will come through
and do justice to the tasks your Son has set us.
Amen.

# The world and the community

# Creation

## Evolution

Creator God,
build up our understanding of your world:
its origins and evolution;
its climatic patterns and changes;
its geology and geography.
But, as we do,
may we step back in wonder
to reflect and give thanks,
to learn from our predecessors
and to praise your works.
Let the footfall of faith be revealed
and renewed in each generation.
We ask this through the light of the world,
your Son, Jesus Christ.
Amen.

Lord of all,
create in us a love and respect
for the origins of your world,
so that all we see we honour,
all we touch we explore,
and all we hear we listen to.
Make us curious to know
the length, depth and height of your generosity
in the life we live,
in the world you made.
May the creative spark that ignited the universe
live in our hearts as well as our minds,
so that our faith grows
as our knowledge is enhanced,
through the one whose love never leaves us,
Jesus Christ.
Amen.

God of nature and nurture,
bring us a greater understanding of how things evolved,
from the dawn of creation,
through the ages of civilisation
to the new millennium.
May we acknowledge and embrace progress
but accept that there may be a cost:
in relationships with each other;
in our relationship with you.
Restore in us the capacity to wonder.
Renew in us the will to believe.
And let us never cease to strive
to leave the world a better place,
just as your Son did, through whom we pray.
Amen.

Lord of nature and nurture,
bring us to a true understanding
of the forces at work in the world,
so that we can build a right relationship with you.
Give us hope and confidence
even when the outlook is bleak.
May we do all we can
to minimise climate change
and to allow your creation
to flourish and evolve
as a sign of your greatness
and as a witness to your love,
evergreen God.
Amen.

# Ecology

Heavenly Father,
you have given us balance and challenge
in the environment we take for granted.
May we learn from our mistakes
in our stewardship and duty of care.
Give us the will and the means
to leave the world a better place,
honouring your gift of the ecology we enjoy.
And in everything we see
let us wonder and give thanks,
offering songs of praise
as well as a witness of silence.
We ask this through your Son, Jesus Christ.
Amen.

Lord of the environment,
may our surroundings be our spur
to honour all that you have created;
to understand the fragile balance of nature;
to be modest in our use of resources;
and to look for fresh ways to conserve energy.
In our prayers as in our loves,
may your Son be our guide
as we seek to follow his ways,
bringing wholeness and healing
instead of partiality and pain,
and letting go of what is not necessary
in our lives and in our hearts.
Amen.

Lord,
our surroundings are your home;
make us houseproud for you.
We thank you for sharing it
with us and all creatures great and small.
Give us an insight into the impact of our actions,
for good and ill, on your world
and on you, forgiving Lord.
Amen.

Wonderful God,
may we never contain our enthusiasm for your creation,
but may we treat all things
as we would treat a neighbour,
and our neighbours as we would treat ourselves,
for all things are of you.
So let our treatment of our environment
be as if we were treating our relationship with you
with integrity, honesty and respect,
knowing that you are immanent and omniscient,
yet sensitive to the needs of the least of your creatures.
Amen.

# Climate

God of contrast and continuity,
bring us rains to refresh and renew;
bring us sun to warm and nurture;
bring us the wind of your Holy Spirit too.
We give thanks for the delicate balance
of the earth's climate and our daily weather.
May we not upset that balance
by trying to do your work, Lord,
but where natural forces impact on your world
let us respond to human need,
using the gifts you provide, generous God.
Amen.

Heavenly Father,
you send the breath of life
through wind and rain and sun.
You send the bread of life
through your only Son.
We give thanks for the climate we depend on,
even when you give us rain
when we want sun.
And even when the snow stops us in our tracks
the weather shows us we can take nothing for granted,
yet have everything to be thankful for,
loving Lord.
Amen.

Almighty God,
ruler of heaven and earth,
who gives us cloud and shade,
who sends us sun and rain,
may we come to appreciate
the sheer variety of climate in the world,
from frozen wastes still harbouring life
to tropical forests helping the earth to breathe.
It is not for us to engineer things, Lord,
but let us also not upset climatic balance
through thoughtless actions and bad stewardship.
Let us be respectful of your creation,
bountiful God.
Amen.

Lord,
as we travel the world and see your creation,
we also feel the differences in climate
between tropical, temperate and polar regions.
We may complain about this at times,
but really we rejoice in the difference and diversity.
Thank you for the opportunities we have
to experience the extremes
without the privations of previous generations.
May those who live in extremes of climate day by day
continue to be sustained by the resilience you have given them.
And may we all be sensitive to the needs of those who cannot cope,
Lord of life.
Amen.

# Natural wonders

Almighty God,
we stand in awe of your works all around us,
the smallest and the greatest.
When we see the mountains in sunlight
we give thanks.
When we watch streams and rivers
we see the living water.
When we hear the birdsong at dawn
we feel so privileged.
Give us an appreciation of your generosity
as we go about our daily round
as well as in our travels afar.
Life is a natural wonder
and you have given us the bread of life,
marvellous God, beneficent Father.
Amen.

Surprising Lord,
who never lets us rest in our journey of life,
open our eyes to the greatness around us.
Help us not to take for granted
that clouds bring rain,
that water brings life,
that the sun brings hope.
Help us safeguard the best of nature,
not just for ourselves
but for future generations.
Give us the patience that you have shown
in giving us a second chance
through your Son, our Saviour,
Jesus Christ.
Amen.

God of power and might,
be gentle with us as we try to scale your mountains,
ride your rivers, fly above your world.
All that you have given us in natural wonders
has pushed the ingenuity and endurance you have also provided
to the limits of our imagination and capacity.
Test us, challenge us, shake us,
so that we can truly appreciate
all you have created
and can take time to thank our creator,
timeless God, eternal Father.
Amen.

God of imagination,
let the natural wonders speak for themselves
of your glory and generosity.
If we reflect on how they were made –
rivers and seas,
mountains and valleys,
stars and galaxies –
we can only give thanks
that we are alive to see them,
able to study them
and have someone to thank for them,
through your Son, our Saviour, Jesus Christ,
Amen.

# Natural disasters

God of mercy,
you have shown through your Son's pain and sacrifice for us
that you share our suffering.
Look with pity and tears
on the struggles of the people of *(name place(s))*
as they try to come to terms with what has befallen them.
May all the energies and expertise of humankind
be extended to those affected,
and may those who suffer and those who mourn
be comforted through your presence with them now.
Amen.

Almighty God,
let the forces unleashed by the *earthquake/flood/eruption* in *(name place(s))*
speak of your power and might.
But may the aftermath testify
to the love you have shown
in sending us your Son.
Let the purpose and resourcefulness
of the survivors and rescuers alike
be united in love for neighbour
and focused on bringing relief and comfort.
May all that you have taught us through your Son
be our motivation and our strength
in responding to need, wherever it shows itself.
And as we do so, Lord,
be alongside the victims in their suffering
and bring hope to their communities.
Amen.

Lord of compassion,
we stand perplexed as we see
the devastation and suffering
in the aftermath of the *(flood/earthquake/eruption)* in *(name place(s))*
We know you are in the midst of the pain,
but help us to understand that you did not unleash
the forces that led to this disaster.
We struggle to comprehend but are ready to act.
Inspire us and all those in the area
to do what we can, in your name,
to take responsibility, as your Son did,
in extending your love to those in need and distress.
Amen.

Heavenly Father,
we need your strength today,
as well as urgency and patience,
in the face of the disaster in *(name place(s))*.
Let the world you created respond,
individually and collectively,
generously and creatively,
to the challenge that faces local communities.
May the worldwide community see it as our responsibility
to help our neighbours as ourselves,
to take comfort from your presence in the midst of suffering
and to direct the skills and resources
where they are really needed,
loving Lord.
Amen.

# Flora and fauna

God of abundance,
you bring the rains and the sun
for the benefit of plants and animals,
as well as for our delight.
May their growth be blessed
and their needs met
without let or hindrance from us,
but with our careful stewardship
of water and irrigation,
of solar and hydro-electric power,
of good gardening and responsible harvesting.
We ask this in your Son's name, Jesus Christ,
Amen.

Lord of light and heat,
let all the creatures and plant life
be blessed in the world of your creation.
Let us not take for granted
that, year after year,
hot summer after hard winter,
life begins again in the year's rotation.
Let us give thanks for this
and give a helping hand to nature
in our tending of plants and nurturing of animals.
May we have green fingers and tender hands
as we look after the natural world
that you have given us and which we must pass on,
Lord of nature and nurture.
Amen.

God of surprise and joy,
may we rejoice in the abundance of flowers
in all sorts of surprising places.
And may we glory in the variety of wildlife,
even in places we may never go.
May we keep our distance
and give space to animals and humans alike,
encourage plant life to flourish,
in gardens and wild places,
keep endangered species safe from harm
and give rare plants a chance to thrive.
We ask this through your Son, Jesus Christ.
Amen.

Gracious God,
who has given us the space and environment
to grow as you would want,
let us not be selfish in our use of your gifts.
Create in us the will and desire
to regard your creatures as our neighbours
and your plant life as our vineyard.
In enjoying your water and your wine,
let us acknowledge that without you
there would be no bread of life,
no living water,
no nourishment
for our faith, our families, our future,
God of life-giving force.
Amen.

# Human society

## Government

God of majesty,
grant those who govern us in this world
the wisdom to do so fairly,
the ability to do so with skill
and the judgement to plan ahead
while responding to immediate need.
Through your Son we have learnt
to render to Caesar what is Caesar's
and we honour you by showing allegiance to government
while working for justice and peace,
as Jesus did.
Amen.

Lord of all,
we are ever grateful for the laws you have given us,
in their stark simplicity.
May we learn the lessons of history
in the way we govern and are governed.
May we elect the leaders we need –
or we are destined to have the leaders we deserve.
Send people with commitment and integrity
to guard us in this world
while you guide us to the next.
We pray for peoples oppressed by dictatorships
and ask that the flame of truth
leads to the warmth of reconciliation,
through your Son, Jesus Christ.
Amen.

Heavenly Father,
bring to our government, local and national,
a renewed drive to empower rather than control,
to serve rather than be served;
may they not flaunt the trappings of status and position.
Let the example of your Son
be the model for our lives
in governing fairly
and obeying proper authority.
But always encourage the gift of prophecy,
today as much as in the age of the great prophets
who foretold the coming of your Son,
Jesus Christ.
Amen.

Almighty God,
you have given us the free will to choose you
and out of grace you have accepted us as your own.
May we learn to use that free will
in our daily round,
to work for what we believe is right in the world,
to vote for those who have the vision
to bring peace, justice and prosperity to an ailing world.
But may we be very mindful
of the love your Son showed
for the marginalised and disenfranchised,
when we seek change in society,
when we elect our political representatives,
when we obey our laws – and yours, gracious God.
Amen.

# Authority

God of power and might,
your authority is absolute
and so very generously applied.
Your laws are strict
and your judgements merciful.
Your vengeance is great
and your reconciliation lasting.
Through your Son you have made all things new.
And from his death on the cross your authority
is transformed through his resurrection
into a new mandate:
to love and be loved
as you love us.
Amen.

Heavenly Father,
we are in awe of you,
yet yearn to know you better.
We thank you that your Son
has shown us a new side to your authority.
May our leaders and governors
learn from his example
in challenging and encouraging,
by example and vision,
through deeds as well as words,
so that we come to respect them,
as we respect the grace and sacrifice
of your only Son, Jesus Christ.
Amen.

All-seeing Lord,
we ask that as you survey your world
you build up the courage of those in authority
to do the right thing;
to know when enough is enough;
to learn from mistakes made;
and to listen to our concerns.
We ask for your blessings on all in authority.
May their judgement be good
and their word their bond.
We ask this through your Son,
whose mercy is without limit
and whose rule is without end.
Amen.

Just and merciful Father,
we build up those in authority –
and bring them down if they fail.
Yet your way is always to forgive
where repentance is sincere
and amendment of life is the outcome.
On a sea of trouble you calm the waters.
So may our leaders react in difficult times
and may all who honour you
treat those under their authority
with justice, with integrity, with mercy.
In the name of the one who loves as you love him,
Jesus Christ.
Amen.

# The sovereign

God who reigns,
bestow your grace and wisdom
on our sovereign, *Queen Elizabeth,*
and all the Royal Family,
so that the responsibilities they have inherited
may be carried out in a way that honours you.
May the Queen's chaplains serve our Governor well
and may *Her* Majesty watch over
the state of the Church
as well as the state of the nation,
with your Son as *her* guide.
We ask this through Jesus Christ.
Amen.

Heavenly Father,
whose rule extends from this kingdom to the next,
bring your blessings on *Elizabeth, our Queen,*
*her* heirs and descendants,
so that *she* may guide *her* subjects well
in all matters spiritual and temporal:
governing your Church and bringing wisdom and experience
to the tasks of prime ministers and governments,
always ready to discern your will
and committed to serve you,
enabling *her* to serve *her* people well,
with the help of Jesus Christ, your Son, our Lord.
Amen.

Almighty God,
who gives us the breath of life
and draws us to himself,
we pray for our sovereign, *Queen Elizabeth,*
as *she* carries out *her* duties.
May she be blessed with the stamina and sensitivity
to respond to all those who seek *her* aid,
the great and the good,
the poor and the marginalised,
the healthy and the suffering,
the government and the governed.
May *she* be blessed with your grace,
supported by her people and drawn to you
when *she* seeks your counsel,
Mighty Counsellor.
Amen.

God of power and majesty,
we ask for your protection and mercy
on our sovereign, *Queen Elizabeth,*
and all the Royal Family.
Bring them insight and judgement
in all their duties and relationships.
And may our *queen* show
that in her governing of your Church
and in her role as head of state
*she* shows the fruits of *her* love for you
and the guidance of her chaplains
as she seeks to be your servant
in serving us, with the help of your Son,
Jesus Christ.
Amen.

# Prayers for council meetings

God of authority and justice,
we ask that the deliberations here
will truly reflect your will.
May all that is said be from deep conviction
and a desire to do the right thing.
May council members be always mindful
of those who elected them
and those whom they serve.
Let disagreement bring new insights;
let challenge provide new answers;
let decisions be based on vision;
and may those who implement what is agreed here
be confident that proper consideration
has been given to the consequences.
In the name of the one whose sacrifice
restored our relationship with you,
Jesus Christ.
Amen.

Heavenly Father,
you wish only for the best for the governance of our affairs.
Pour down on this council your grace and wisdom
so that issues are explored fully,
people are listened to as well as heard,
and there is adequate understanding of the decisions and outcomes.
Bring healthy debate and proper scrutiny
to all that is said and done here.
And may those who disagree
have the consolation of free speech to make their views known.
We ask this through the one who respected authority
in this world and the next,
your Son, Jesus Christ.
Amen.

Lord God,
who rules with justice and mercy,
watch over our council meeting.
Let judgement and discernment be evident
in all the discussions and in the decisions taken.
May principles be to the fore,
whatever the political viewpoint.
But also let reconciliation and fairness reign,
so that implementation and outcomes
are properly understood and scrupulously carried out.
May the council show wisdom and courage,
as you would want, creative God.
Amen.

Almighty God,
as we gather for the business of council,
let us remember those the council serves
and those who serve the council.
May we always know the limitations,
as well as the powers, of this body.
In exercising the council's responsibility,
grant to members the energy and commitment
to be true to your purpose for us,
so that we may be confident
in our accountability to the community,
to the *(town/city/district)* of *(name)*
and to you, who will judge us all.
Amen.

# War and conflict

Lord God,
you use your power and might with restraint and judgement.
Let justice and mercy guide our armed forces,
whether they are defending us
or keeping the peace around the world.
We pray for trouble spots and war zones
where war and conflict are rife.
Bring resolutions to these struggles
through discussion and negotiation where possible
and through force only where necessary to restore peace
as your Son would.
Amen.

God of peace,
watch over those who guard our nation
and those who protect the defenceless and vulnerable.
May we never glorify war,
even where conflict is unavoidable.
Let mercy accompany justice
and restraint accompany force.
And may we always remember
those who die or sustain injuries
in the heat of combat,
in support of each other,
in defending our liberty,
in overcoming oppression.
Lest we forget.
Amen.

Lord of all,
create in us a propensity for peace
rather than a desire for conflict.
But where war is just
and oppression must be confronted,
give to our armed forces the gift of wisdom
and the quality of mercy.
Let them be safe in their professionalism,
be led well in the field
and show respect for victims and vanquished alike.
We give thanks for risks taken
and lives lost on our behalf,
never forgetting that your Son died for us.
Amen.

God of justice and mercy,
we pray for war zones across the world;
for those caught up in conflicts,
innocent bystanders
as well as armed service professionals.
May the leaders of countries and factions
take stock of the consequences, intended and unintended,
of prolonged conflicts or acts of violence.
May freedom fighters forgo acts of terrorism
and official armies avoid excessive force.
May your love break through tensions and impasse,
preventing further loss of life and limb,
encouraging negotiation and reconciliation
and liberating civilians and combatants alike.
We ask this in Jesus' name.
Amen.

# Peace and reconciliation

Reconciling Lord,
may peace flourish where once there was conflict
and may reconciliation grow in the hearts of those involved.
Bring your blessings on the peacemakers
and also on the sustainers of hope.
Let all who know your love
share it with friends and foes alike,
following your Son's example
of selfless giving and sacrifice.
Lord of all mercy, we ask this
in the name of Jesus Christ.
Amen.

God of power and peace,
let those who seek war and conflict
always try to find another way,
your way, to resolve disputes,
and resort to armed conflict
only where justice and liberty are at stake.
Bring to the hearts and minds of leaders and led,
victors and victims,
a deep desire for peace
and a strong commitment to resolution and reconciliation
when the fighting's done,
and the requirements of peace
bring new responsibilities:
no easy way, as your Son knows.
Amen.

God of mercy,
you set captives free
and made all things new
through your Son's service and sacrifice.
Pour down on the lands where there is armed struggle
that special grace for peace
so that fires are extinguished,
hatred turned to love,
and the still, small voice of calm
brings a commitment to reconciliation
and the promise of a new dawn,
through your Son, Jesus Christ.
Amen.

Loving Lord, giving God,
send peace,
bring calm,
sow seeds of love,
show olive branches,
create hope,
move mountains,
nurture reconciliation,
love, love
and love again,
that we might live in the light of Christ.
Amen.

# Hunger and thirst

Lord, giver of life,
your Son shared with us the bread of life.
May we play our part in sharing that bread
to meet the needs of the hungry and thirsty,
both spiritually and materially,
by listening and looking,
by responding and planning,
by mobilising and encouraging,
and above all, Lord, through prayer.
Help us to be persistent and insistent,
knowing that your Son sacrificed all through his commitment
to make all things new.
Amen.

Lord of all,
we pray for the hungry in our world,
in continents where hunger is widespread
and in parts of our land where deprivation persists.
Let us not stereotype or marginalise,
knowing that your Son never did.
Every human is special in your eyes
and should be in ours too.
May those who thirst receive the clean water they deserve,
and you have provided, if only we can ensure
that water is available and drinkable,
by using the gifts you have given us, gracious God.
Amen.

Inclusive God,
who blesses the hungry with good things,
if we heed your call and share your world,
may we never forget our basic humanity
in a rush for material progress.
Let us realise the limitations of possessions,
but also the power of your gifts to us,
in whatever form we can use them:
our skills and abilities – bless them;
our relationships with others – develop them;
our resources and knowledge – distribute them.
Wherever and whenever we encounter hunger and thirst,
may we have a right judgement about our response,
in the name of Jesus Christ, who fed the five thousand.
Amen.

Heavenly Father,
who brings us the rain and sun
which make the soil and sea so abundant
in life-giving food that sustains us in body:
may our souls also be nourished by your gift of life
through struggle and service
but also in our worship and praise.
May we always be open to new insights into your way
of feeding our needs and spreading your love.
But, most of all, help us to see
the link between the body and the spirit,
so that in meeting one need
we feed another, as your Son did.
Amen.

# Riches and generosity

Lord of all,
you have given us riches indeed
to use and share,
not hoard and hide.
May we put those gifts to your service,
material and spiritual,
practical and emotional,
so that we can truly reflect
the generosity you have shown to us
in sending your Son, Jesus Christ.
Amen.

God of power and might,
may we learn from the story of Dives
and from your Son's advice to the young lawyer,
so that, not out of fear but out of love for you,
we may not be governed by material things.
May our treasures be in our hearts and in our actions,
and may we be generous in those actions,
however small or large to us,
knowing that it is in the ordinary
that the extraordinary can be revealed.
Give us, we ask, the insight and the will
to make a difference to the lives of others,
through the love your Son showed us.
Amen.

Father of all,
you have showered us with the fruits of your creation.
May we reciprocate with our praises and prayers.
Let the generosity you have shown to us
be a spur and an inspiration to all your people.
Bring us to share the promise of salvation.
Bring us to experience the blessing of your forgiveness.
Bring us to a proper understanding of your love
and then challenge us, Lord,
to pass on the richness of your generosity
to future generations, through learning and listening
as well as teaching and encouraging.
Amen.

Extravagant God,
empower us with the spirit of generosity,
so that we may give of our time, our talents, and ourselves
to your service and glory,
in the little, unremembered acts of kindness and love,
and in the public square of challenge and controversy.
Arm us with the determination and zeal
to put principle before material gain
and to encourage those with resources
beyond our wildest dreams
to direct them to the fullness of your kingdom,
with the help of Jesus Christ, your Son.
Amen.

# Community

## Local community

Lord of all,
bring us a real sense of community
in our villages and towns, our cities and suburbs.
And may that extend from our homes to our streets,
to our places of work and places of study.
May the God that draws us together to worship in church
continue in our daily lives,
so that we can be good neighbours
and good stewards of our neighbourhoods,
through the love of him who brings healing and wholeness,
your Son, Jesus Christ.
Amen.

God of friendship and hope,
in our community
may we cherish new friendships and new neighbours,
as well as sustaining long-standing relationships.
Your apostles blazed a trail of bringing the good news.
May we, through hospitality and courtesy,
witness to the love that you have showed us
in sending us your Son,
who made all things new
and rescued our relationship with you,
God of mercy and restoration.
Amen.

Almighty God,
who brings out the extraordinary in the ordinary,
we thank you for the joy
of greeting friends and neighbours;
of sharing meals in homes and halls;
of helping out and being helped;
of playing and listening to music together;
of honouring difference and celebrating diversity;
of joining together to worship you,
God of community – and all communities.
Amen.

God of subsidiarity,
you have given us free will
to be set apart or in community,
to be independent or interdependent.
May we never seek to be anything but dependent on you
for our creation, preservation
and for guiding our relationships with each other
in our *(village/suburb/town/city).*
And may there always be room in our hearts for you,
as there was not at the inn that turned away
the mother of your Son,
Jesus Christ.
Amen.

# Networks

Lord of relationships,
thank you for reconnecting us to you through your Son.
Restore to us a true sense of place and purpose.
May our links with each other bring us a sense of community
by shared purpose, joint interest,
and a desire to explore all aspects of your world.
Let our networks be to your glory
and may we never forget
that these networks are only possible
because you gave us the free will
to live our lives in the light of your Son,
who always wants the best from us,
in the associations we have
and the relationships we make.
Amen.

Heavenly Father,
help us to depend on each other,
in our lives, in our work, in our leisure interests.
And may the networks we form
never stray far from you,
who created the network of stars and light
that give us life and breath.
And may we build networks in our lives
which speak of you and witness to you
in how we communicate;
in how we show respect;
in how we love neighbour as self;
in how we respond to need.
Let us embrace the technology of change,
as your Son transformed our relationship with you,
Sovereign God.
Amen.

God of gifts and generosity,
help us to rise to the challenge of change
in our communities as in our lives.
May our relationships be enhanced
through new means of communication,
so that we can be in touch in new and exciting ways,
not limited to occasional meetings,
not limited by time and space,
enriching our communications for a purpose.
And may we seek new ways
of developing our relationship with you, Lord,
to enhance our worship in church,
to acknowledge your presence in all we do
and in every medium and network
you have given for our use,
immanent Lord.
Amen.

Lord God,
be in our words
as we talk to each other.
Be in our hearts
as we care for one another.
Be in our eyes
as we seek to understand others.

Be in our imagination
as we catch a glimpse of your vision.
Be in our joy
as we see growth and development in family and friends.
Be in our compassion
as we share the suffering around us.

Be in our hope
as we hear your Son's promises.
Be in our networks of faith
as we try to be good disciples.
Be with us, without end.
Amen.

# Education and learning

Almighty God,
we ask that we can be a learning community,
getting to know you more and more,
learning to love you as you love us,
growing in faith together,
worshipping as if our life depends on you,
because it does.
We ask this in the name of Jesus Christ, our Lord.
Amen.

Teacher,
give us the will to do our best
for young people in our care,
to go the extra mile for their sake,
to equip them for a life of learning,
and to foster in them a love for your creation.
May we always seek to widen horizons,
not lower sights,
and to let challenge and risk be seen
as opportunities to be negotiated,
under our watchful eye and your pastoral care.
Break down barriers to knowledge
and unlock the creativity you have given us
to enjoy the gifts you have provided
and to be good stewards of the resources you have given.
Amen

Lord,
we ask for your blessing on schools in our community,
on the headteachers and staff, governors and pupils.
Give them the love of learning and the gift of teaching
so that the teaching can bear fruit
in ways that please you
and bring smiles of appreciation to pupils and parents.
May there be good links
between home and school,
school and church,
church and community,
so that there can be joint celebration in good times
and care and support in difficult times,
as your Son, Jesus Christ, would wish.
Amen.

God of challenge and change,
may we nurture the gifts of the new generation,
as well as acknowledge the contribution of past generations.
Help our schools, colleges and universities
as they build up the body of knowledge
and its applications for today and tomorrow.
May there be a right balance between affirmation and judgement,
encouragement and strictures,
so that standards in all aspects of life can be high,
but those who do not measure up
can always rely on the same love and care
that your Son showed to those
who had least or suffered most.
Thank you, Lord.
Amen.

# Youth and uniformed groups

God of inspiration and aspiration,
we ask for your blessings on the youth of today
and on the people and organisations
who give them opportunities to grow.
Let the uniformed organisations flourish in our halls and churches
and let leaders come forward
to continue to develop the work
in every generation.
Help us to trust and let go,
as well as organise and oversee.
Above all, may there be fun and fellowship
alongside the challenges met, the badges won,
and the friendships made.
Amen.

Father of all,
help all those involved with young people
to bring aspiration and understanding,
to equip for future achievement,
to promote responsibility and faith in the future,
and not to dwell on what might have been.
May uniformed organisations build up individual potential
as well as team endeavour.
May the Scouts and Venture Scouts, Guides and Rangers,
Cubs and Brownies, Rainbows and Beavers
all be blessed with committed leaders,
encouraging parents and firm friendships,
so that communities can be built up
and lasting relationships forged.
Amen.

Heavenly Father,
may our churches be blessed with strong groups of young people,
from toddler groups to youth groups,
from junior church to choirs and music groups.
May we always see them as part of *today's* church,
knowing that if we fail to do this
we ignore the future by dwelling on the past.
May we see the present as a gift to be cherished,
an opportunity not to be missed,
as we grow discipleship
in the young of today,
from whom we have so much to learn,
as your Son showed us.
Amen.

God of community,
let young and old, children and adults,
play a full part in all aspects of our lives,
in our church communities, our homes and neighbourhoods,
our networks and prayers.
May we always be aware of differing needs and potential skills.
As your Son directed the disciples
to let children have access to him,
so may we seek to include rather than exclude
when we look to meet the needs of young people.
Above all, Lord, bring us the gift of discernment
as young people seek your purpose for them.
Amen.

# On the edge

## The marginalised

Lord of the unloved,
help us to be more like you,
to include where we would tend to exclude;
to recognise gifts instead of faults;
to seek out those on the edge of society;
and to bring wholeness to the broken in spirit.
Your Son has showed us the way,
in his reaching out and his bringing in.
Let us be open and welcoming,
even when we feel challenged and uncomfortable.
We ask you to strengthen our resolve
and equip us to be gracious and accepting
in all our doings in this world,
as you are to us, God of grace.
Amen.

God of vision and understanding,
may we always seek to know you in the stranger;
may we listen to you in the bystander;
may we recognise you in the timid and tender.
Give us all the courage of a faith
which looks to your Son as a model,
to your Holy Spirit as the enabler,
and to you for our creation and preservation.
You have given us difference and diversity.
Let us seek to embrace and get to know the differences,
so that we can better understand the whole of your world
and the extent of your love for all,
through your Son, who shows us the way.
Amen.

Almighty God,
You can shape our future as you have shaped our past.
Bring us wisdom to know our limitations
as well as the gifts of others.
May we see you in unlikely places and people.
May we learn from those who seem to have no stake in society.
Give us insight and discernment
as we try to encourage, enable and equip,
not only through skills and qualities we have been given,
but also through an awareness and humility
which we can sustain
only with the help of your Son, Jesus Christ.
Amen.

Heavenly Father,
you have given us a big issue to work on,
showing us abundance of riches
alongside deprivation and poverty.
Put us in the shoes (if they have them)
of those our society shuns.
Put us in the minds
of the broken in health and spirit.
Put us in the hearts
of those who hurt and who are hurt by others.
Give us, we pray, the 'inside out' understanding
to turn the world upside down, as your Son did,
meeting you in our encounters with the downtrodden;
encountering our real selves
in our meetings with the marginalised.
Amen.

# The excluded

Lord of all,
you embrace all of humanity,
enfolding us in love and grace.
Teach us to open our hearts
to those at the margins of society,
because that is where you are,
and where we should be too.
We thank you for the many gifts and benefits of life,
but, in gratitude and thanksgiving,
we know we fall short of your generosity.
Your Son taught us the way of inclusiveness.
Help us to see the truth of his teaching
so that we can lead the life he wants us to lead,
through Jesus Christ.
Amen.

God of mercy, God of grace,
keep us to the true path;
not one that constrains and ignores those by the wayside,
but the true path that keeps us alert
to all that happens along the way;
to those who are resting;
to those who are suffering;
to those who are hiding;
to those who are being kept from us – and from you.
Let us always seek ways to open hearts
and to open doors, for you to come to us,
and for us to go out,
whenever you call,
wherever that leads.
God of adventure, we thank you.
Amen.

Heavenly Father,
you came down in your Son,
to include us in your kingdom.
May we respond by inviting all to join you:
the well-heeled and privileged
who may need to learn humility;
the poor and marginalised
who need to know you care;
and ourselves, with all our imperfections.
You can make all things new,
so we ask that you turn things upside down
and inside out,
as we answer your Son's call to welcome the stranger
and to learn from the outsider,
so that the excluded feel part of your kingdom
and special in your eyes.
Amen.

Immanent Lord,
creator of the outer reaches of the universe
as well as the stars nearer home,
bring us to realise that you are in all humanity,
rich, poor, gay, straight, black, white;
and your Church is for all ages,
all backgrounds, all states of grace.
Give us the courage and the means
to welcome where once we turned away,
to love where once we hated,
to support where once we walked away.
Let your Holy Spirit work within us,
to help us appreciate all that is around us,
inclusive Lord.
Amen.

# The stranger

God of friendship,
your Son showed us the meaning of hospitality
towards disciples and strangers alike.
May we, like him, offer a hand of welcome
and a sign of friendship
when we meet strangers in our neighbourhood or church,
just as we would hope for the same
when we are strangers in other places.
But whatever our own experience,
let us be good hosts to strangers,
not because we expect to earn our own welcome
but because your Son has shown us, and you guide us,
to do always what is right in your sight.
Amen.

Lord and Father of humankind,
you sent your Son as a stranger in a hostile world:
born in an outhouse,
shunned by ordinary people
and killed by the great and the good.
Only the excluded, the outcast,
faithful fishermen and loyal womenfolk,
welcomed him and took him to their hearts
as the prophets would have wanted.
So let us learn our lessons and free our hearts
to be accepting of the stranger,
to be open to the different,
to be gracious to the alien,
to be generous to grateful and ungrateful alike.
Help us to be a bit more like your Son,
whose welcome is constant to those who turn to him.
Amen.

Lord of light,
shine your beam of positive energy
on all of us in our dealings with strangers.
May we beware of those who mean us harm,
but let us trust our instincts and your direction
when we come across those who need your love.
May we discern their inner feelings
and seek to engage with people in a spirit of empathy.
Grow in us, Lord, a sense of trust,
a tendency to listen as well as hear,
and a willingness to be challenged,
as your Son was.
Amen.

God of great expectations,
pour down on your people
a generosity of spirit which breaks down barriers.
Create in us the capacity
to grow in faith in you
and to have more faith in other people,
in particular those we don't know,
but whom we meet in different situations.
May we incline our hearts to them
rather than turn our backs on them.
Give us the trust in you
and the confidence in ourselves
to take risks in getting to know strangers
and to be ready to learn new things
from people we may neither know nor like.
Send us out in the Spirit that sent your Son into the world
and the Spirit that lives with us now.
Amen.

# The different

God of great generosity,
look at the sheer diversity of your creation
and help us to celebrate differences.
In our heart of hearts we know the importance of difference,
yet sometimes we ignore or shun the different.
May we embrace diversity,
cherish, encourage and challenge other ways,
and not be afraid of 'the other'.
Take away our distrust of what we are not used to
and make us open to the shock of the new,
as well as the legacy of the past,
even as we make the most of the present.
We ask this through the one
who both acknowledged difference and ignored it,
your Son, Jesus Christ,
Amen.

Dear Lord,
make it our pleasure and responsibility
to bring an openness of spirit
to all our encounters with those we meet.
In our places of work,
in our houses and in our churches,
may we be available to others,
slow to judge,
and quick to respond to need.
May we offer the gift of hospitality,
as we have received it so many times ourselves,
from strangers and friends,
from family and neighbours,
from your Son, via his disciples,
and directly to us, generous God.
Amen.

God of greatness and mercy,
your Son always saw the best in people
and forgave those who repented their worst.
Help us to respect those who are different from us,
acknowledging that we are all different and special in your eyes.
Give us the empathy and the interest
to communicate well with others,
making fresh connections and sharing our common humanity.
Develop our insights and strengthen our resolve
to love others as you love us.
Amen.

Great Shepherd of the sheep,
may we be both pastor and friend
to those of a different ethnic origin,
to those of a different sexuality,
to those of a different age,
to those of a different faith,
to those of a different nationality.
As you are alongside the lonely and oppressed,
the minority as well as the majority,
help us to make room in our hearts
to get to know the different in your world,
because we all share in one bread,
the bread of life.
Amen.

# Minorities

God of the downtrodden,
you know through your Son
what it is to be the minority,
not only through his own persecution and suffering,
but through his rapport with the oppressed and outcast.
We ask that we are strengthened
in our sensitivity to those in a similar situation,
whether through background, status, position or sexual orientation.
Let majorities understand their special responsibility
not to impose their will
but to follow you,
generous and inclusive Lord.
Amen.

Heavenly Father,
to you everyone is special – and all are different.
Help us, where we are in the majority,
to be generous and gracious to minorities.
Help us, where we are in the minority,
to appreciate the needs and aspirations of the many.
In both cases may we seek to make our contribution,
in the knowledge and assurance of your kingdom,
in the hope and faith of the disciples.
May our own discipleship
be strong enough to resist bullying and condemn oppression,
with your help.
Amen.

Lord of all,
of small and large, strong and weak,
of great numbers and single figures,
may we respect minorities when we are in the majority
and respect majorities when we are part of a minority.
May we never forget that all of us change
from majority to minority and back
according to our role.
Let us take our cue from your Son's championing of minorities,
from the Good Samaritan to the tax collector,
from the leper to the prostitute,
from children to the hungry.
Thank you for his example,
through whom we pray, Jesus Christ.
Amen.

God of greatness,
you know that small is beautiful too.
As we appreciate the infinitesimal
alongside the universal,
and recognise the extraordinary in the ordinary,
so may we cherish any minority,
however strong or fragile,
gentle or vociferous,
and seek always to do your will
in the way we respond to their cries
and the way we understand their needs.
But just as warlike might is not always right,
so we should use judgement and fairness
in responding to demands from minorities,
showing the justice your Son did not receive
from the great and the good.
Amen.

# The prejudiced

Forgiving Lord,
help us in our prejudice.
May we constantly be aware
of all that causes us to dislike others.
Show us the way to love others,
even when we can't bring ourselves to like them.
Give us the insight to understand others;
give us the grace to respect others;
and even where we still feel envious or diminished
may we learn from the example of your Son,
who faced prejudice and hate,
resentment and betrayal,
to save us from our sins – including prejudice.
Amen.

Lord of all,
extend your love to those consumed by hate.
Help them to look at the origins of prejudice
so that they can tackle whatever troubles them.
May they be able to turn from resentment
to the path of dialogue and discussion,
resisting the temptation to stoke up hatred.
May your will break through prejudice and pride
to bring healing and help where needed,
even if your love is resisted and rejected,
as your Son was, in order for our relationship with you
to be restored – for good.
Amen.

Heavenly Father,
you know our innermost thoughts
and all our imperfections.
Create in us all a desire to reduce and eliminate prejudice:
prejudice against you;
prejudice against fellow humans;
prejudice against other countries;
prejudice against those who do things differently from us;
prejudice against the old or the young;
prejudice against those who seek the truth.
Empower and enable those who confront prejudice,
and those who seek to mediate and reconcile,
with patience, perseverance
and the power of the Holy Spirit,
to make a difference in your name.
Amen.

God of great change,
pour the power of your transforming love
on those entrenched in prejudice and pride.
May they learn the lessons of history
where ignorance has bred suspicion,
leading to resentment and envy,
hatred and violence.
Give us all the capacity to work through our frustrations,
improve our sense of right and wrong,
and set an example of openness and acceptance
in our dealings with victims and oppressors alike,
while condemning the prejudice as it shows itself.
Give us the strength to make a stand,
with the help of Jesus Christ, your Son,
our Saviour.
Amen.

# Health and pastoral

# Life and living

Lord of life,
bring hope and abundant life
to your people, your creation.
May we always walk with you;
may we always celebrate with you;
may we join with you in the sheer wonder of life.
Help us to appreciate there is a time for joy
and a time for heartache,
but that in all that befalls us
you are there in our elation
and in the depths of sorrow,
as you were there at Easter,
but also on Good Friday.
Amen.

Almighty God,
you know our going out and coming in,
our sorrows and joys,
our highs and lows.
We thank you for the priceless gift of life,
which we your servants sometimes take for granted
even when we see the miracle of a newborn child,
experience the exhilaration of sporting achievement,
or the spirituality of musical yearning.
Give us those visionary moments of life-enhancing brilliance
to tide us over the despondency of failure.
Help us always to learn as we go,
giving thanks to you along the way.
Amen.

God of amazement and joy,
may we never stop praising you:
for the life you give us
and the living we experience;
in our daily round
and in our great adventures.
Help us to savour the special moments,
to help others celebrate theirs,
and to create within us the capacity to hope
and the ability to share happiness and sadness,
elation and depression;
so that at the last we can truly say
that we have lived life to the full,
abundantly and creatively, knowing you
and following the example of your Son, Jesus Christ.
Amen.

Loving, living Lord,
let all who hear your name
join in a joyful song.
We give thanks for the sheer delight of life,
not just our own, but in common with all life around:
our family, friends and neighbours,
our pets and all the flora and fauna in our habitat.
May we only connect with all your creatures
so that we can truly be ourselves;
so that we can have a right relationship with you;
and so that in all we experience
we can thank you, creator of all.
Amen.

# Illness and healing

Healing, loving Lord,
be with those who are suffering
through sickness, distress or depression.
Calm and comfort them
and give the peace only you can provide.
May those who care for and minister to them
be given strength and patience.
May the medical and nursing professions
be graced with a concern for the whole person,
just as your Son always was
when healing the sick and forgiving sins.
May hope bring healing
and healing bring wholeness.
Amen.

Lord of all,
we know you neither bring suffering
nor ignore the pain and distress of illness.
But we give thanks and pray for
your continued, comforting presence
alongside the sick and the injured.
Awaken in those who are unwell,
and in those who care for others,
a love for fellow humans
to match your own.
Your Son has always been our model and guide.
Let us be inspired by the miracles of his healing
as well as the tears he shed
for the sick and bereaved.
We ask this through the one who suffered for us,
your Son, Jesus Christ.
Amen.

Caring Lord,
we pray for those in our church community
who are in urgent need of our prayers at this time.
For the sick: bring them healing;
for the injured: bring them swift recovery;
for the depressed: bring them hope;
for the bereaved: bring them comfort.
We ask that in the depths of suffering
they find the well-spring of your grace,
and that in the process of recovery
they find the warmth of caring love,
from family, friends, neighbours,
and above all from you,
God of consolation.
Amen.

God of comfort,
bring to us all, in sickness and in health,
an appreciation of the needs of those who suffer and those who care.
May we be the first to help and the last to leave
when we are faced with the needs of others.
And may we be the first to ask for help
when we ourselves are in urgent need.
As givers and receivers,
may we always offer thanks to you
and ask for the inspiration and resilience
to help in the healing process,
to recognise the skills of others,
to be grateful for our own gifts,
and to respond without hesitation
to the call of the Holy Spirit
in testing situations of life and death.
Amen.

# Suffering and loss

God of compassion,
bring your comfort and your loving presence
to all those who are suffering at this time:
for the injured and all in pain;
for the sick and the troubled;
for the bereaved and lonely.
May your love show itself
through the care of your people
as well as the comfort of your Holy Spirit.
We ask these things through your Son, Jesus Christ,
who suffers with us and suffered for us.
Amen.

Lord God,
who never seeks or encourages suffering,
be with the victims and perpetrators of violence
and bring comfort and reconciliation
wherever these are needed,
in families and dictatorships,
in wars and peacekeeping exercises,
in bullying relationships,
and in places of work.
May our churches and our homes
be sanctuaries of peace and calm.
And may we seek your strength
to go the extra step, the extra mile;
to show your compassion
through our own efforts to help;
and to mobilise the support of others
to be good disciples and faithful followers.
Amen.

God of hope,
help those who suffer to be resilient:
help them to look forward, not back;
and bring them relief from pain
in their bodies and in their hearts,
knowing your presence in their lives,
and sensing your own tears as they shed theirs.
As we pray especially for *(name(s))*
give us the insights and the empathy
to say and do the right things,
in your sight and theirs, Lord.
And when we are in pain and grief ourselves,
let us not blame others – or you.
Let us seek the support of family and friends;
let us trust those with professional skills and knowledge;
and let us continue to worship and give thanks to you,
merciful God, loving Lord.
Amen.

Lord of life,
when death strikes,
let us mourn the person,
let us remember the character,
let us rejoice in the achievements,
let us acknowledge the legacy.
But help us also to wish the soul well
in your new-found presence in the eternal kingdom,
where one day we will all be,
if it is your will,
by your grace and your Son's sacrifice.
We pray for those who still grieve,
both for recent losses of loved ones
and for losses that still hurt
after many years of separation.
Bring us all closer to you,
as your Son did – and still does.
Amen.

# Love and hope

Lord of all hopefulness,
grant to us a glimpse of your eternal love:
in our appreciation of your creation;
in our love for one another;
in the silence of nature;
in the music that enfolds us;
in the house and in the family.
May our churches be places of celebration and real repentance,
so that our spirits are lifted
as we praise your name;
and our commitment redoubled
to spread your name far and wide,
knowing that you will equip us for our journey,
with the help of your Son, our Saviour, Jesus Christ.
Amen.

Almighty God,
give us your strength and the power of your love,
not just for ourselves
but in our dealings with others,
in your name and armed with the Holy Spirit,
to bring us to a knowledge of salvation
and an understanding of hope.
Your Son showed the way of truth and the path of righteousness.
Give us that purpose and peace
to entrust you with our lives, our fears,
our loves, our losses,
but, above all, with our joy and praise
to carry us home to you.
Amen.

Loving God,
you give us hope in all its fullness;
in our faith in the future,
in our cherishing of the present,
in the lessons from the past.
Let your love shine through that hope,
so that people may see the light in our lives
and receive the light in theirs.
We give thanks for all those
who have influenced our own lives,
through example, inspiration, consolation and love,
especially through your Son, Jesus Christ.
Amen.

Heavenly Father,
your love knows no bounds,
so we give you our thanks.
Your hope lifts our spirits
so we give you our hearts.
Your Son saved us from our sins
so we give you our souls.
Your world gives us life
so we live life abundantly.
May we live in peace,
love in peace,
hope in peace
and rest in peace.
Amen.

# Beginnings and endings

# Birth

Lord of new beginnings,
we thank you for the gift of new birth,
with all the hopes and expectations of life.
May we always be aware of how precious,
how special, and how extraordinary
is the miracle of that first breath.
You are there, in the ordinary and everyday,
in the comings and goings of our lives.
But let us celebrate those special moments
when the world stops and a baby is born.
Give us the capacity to rejoice
as those who have gone before have done,
remembering the birth of your Son, Jesus Christ.
Amen.

Lord of hope,
create in us a sense of eternity
through the miracle of a newborn child.
We ask for your blessings on the start of a new journey,
with all the potential to be realised,
all the care to be received and offered,
and the faith to be nurtured and shared.
Give us the responsibility to always be ready to respond
to the cry for help and the leap of joy.
And may we always be mindful
of the impact of our actions and example
on the heart and soul of a young person,
as your Son taught us, in his words and deeds.
Amen.

Amazing God,
you always surprise us through the beauty of your creation,
both the nature of our world and the gift of life.
Help us to comprehend, in our wonder,
the length, breadth and depth of your love
that brings us a new reason for being,
a fresh impression of your bounty.
Let the light that your Son brought into the world
shine in the face of every newborn child.
Let the darkness that threatens us
be held at bay and not hold sway.
And may we all light a candle
for the hearts and minds of those who go astray,
in the sure and certain hope
that there is a new creation,
through your Son, our Saviour, Jesus Christ.
Amen.

God of great hope and new birth,
watch over your new child *(name)*,
who has been brought safely into the world,
the apple of your eye and *his* parents'.
Keep *him* safe in the shadow of your wings
and at the heart of your purpose.
Give to us all the will and responsibility
to nurture and develop *his* life in the love of God.
And, in due course, may we trust and let go,
knowing that you are always there,
in good times and bad,
for us all to lean on,
Father, Son and Holy Spirit,
ever three, ever one.
Amen.

# Baptism

Welcoming God,
we ask that through the christening of *(name)*
we all renew our baptismal vows,
our commitment to do your will,
the repentance of our sins,
redeemed by your Son,
and our rejection of the devil
and the forces of darkness.
May we cherish and nurture this new member of your Church
and make every effort to help *her*
to pray as your Son taught us,
to be a good neighbour,
and to walk humbly with you, our God.
Amen.

God of giant steps,
look down with favour on the tiny steps taken by *(name)*
as *he* is welcomed by this church, your Church,
and as we commit our support individually and collectively
to *his* faith journey,
which starts today and continues tomorrow,
full of hope, full of promise.
May we give thanks for his presence
and pray for the future before *him.*
Guard and guide *him* all the days of *his* life.
Amen.

Dear Lord,
the giver of good things,
may the blessings of the baptismal water
sprinkle over all our lives,
washing and refreshing,
making new and making good.
Inspire us with new responsibility
as we welcome *(name)* into your Church.
May we gather round in love and celebration
as we enfold *(name)* in our arms.
May *she* always be in our hearts too,
and may your Holy Spirit enrich the life you have given,
feed the soul which yearns for you,
Gracious God, eternal deity.
Amen.

All-seeing God, protector and friend,
keep safe your child *(name)*
as we mark this christening
with baptismal waters which remind us of the Jordan;
with the blessing of the Holy Spirit
which reminds us of the dove descending;
and with the acceptance of responsibility
by priests, godparents and all of us present,
to nurture *his* faith,
to care for *him* personally,
to watch over *him* spiritually,
and to mentor his discipleship
in the journey before *him.*
We ask this for the sake of your Son, Jesus Christ.
Amen.

# Confirmation

Affirming Lord,
grant to your candidate(s) the openness to grow in faith,
so that your Holy Spirit shows itself
in action and word,
in sacrament and prayer,
in repentance and forgiveness.
May the sharing of the bread and the wine
be seen as a blessing and a symbol
of the body and blood of your Son.
And may every Eucharist
be a thanksgiving and a self-giving,
a breaking and a shedding,
but unifying us in you,
through your Son, Jesus Christ.
Amen.

God of trust and empowerment,
launch your candidate(s) on to the sea of faith,
sure of their navigation,
always looking to the stars,
relying on their compasses along the way,
and trusting in your support in rough seas.
Give to all those keen to know you better
the gift of exploring and deepening their faith,
so that they can glimpse the mind of God,
through the taking of the wine and the bread,
as a timeless reminder of the sacrifices your Son suffered,
not just for humankind as a whole,
but for you and me.
Amen.

Forgiving, giving God,
take your candidate(s) into the heart and soul of faith,
so that in receiving the bread and the wine
they may see the bread as your Son's body, broken for us,
and may know the wine as your Son's blood, shed for us.
May the mystery of faith become clearer,
so that hearts are warmed with your Holy Spirit,
and minds are filled with wonder and understanding,
a wisdom born of knowledge
but matured in relationship
with your Son, our Saviour, Jesus Christ.
Amen.

Lord of light,
awaken in your servant(s)
a growing sense of you in their heart(s);
a desire to know the Holy Spirit in their faith journey;
a wonder at your creation in their eyes;
a love for their neighbours in their actions;
a knowledge of your presence in the breaking of the bread;
an appreciation of your Son's sacrifice in the sharing of the wine.
And may they walk in your ways
as long as they live(s),
faithful Father, loving Lord.
Amen.

# Weddings

Lord of life and love,
pour down your blessings on *(name)* and *(name).*
May they grow in understanding and trust
as they embark on their future life together.
May the bonds that unite them
be strong enough to resist the temptations to stray.
And may they be all the stronger
for the love and affection from all around on this wedding day.
Give them the heart and soul
to show, in their love for one another,
a selflessness and caring concern
which shine out as a beacon of hope
and a reflection of your love for them,
gracious God.
Amen.

Bringer of peace and love,
we pray for couples approaching their wedding day,
for the careful preparation of practical arrangements,
but also in getting ready for the emotional and spiritual challenges
that the day itself will bring.
Give patience and perseverance to all concerned
and make the whole experience of the wedding
worthy of the occasion,
worthy of you, Lord,
and special in the eyes of all who attend.
May wedding days be feast days
for all involved – and for you too, Lord,
God of purpose and destiny.
Amen.

Father of all,
your love stretches to your whole creation,
yet also to each individual family.
Grant *(name)* and *(name)* the favour of your presence,
in their love, in their lives,
on this special day.
Let the heavens rejoice with you
to see these two pledge their faithfulness
to each other, to the solemn vows of marriage
and to a future together, under your protection.
Give them the strength to persevere
when times get tough
and the time and space together
to get to know each other day by day,
in the hope of Christ.
Amen.

Heavenly Father,
we gather to witness the union of *(name)* and *(name)*
before you, before the world,
in the midst of shared love,
and in the shining light of your approval.
May they gain the knowledge of the hope and inspiration
that comes from a true appreciation
of the holy state of matrimony,
the highs and lows of life together,
the prospect of children,
if that is your will, Lord,
and, above all, the gift of sharing,
the wonder of love,
and the promise of your presence
whenever they need the reassurance
and reconciliation of your Son, Jesus Christ.
Amen.

# Family

Lord of young and old,
we give thanks for family,
for the wisdom of age,
and the enthusiasm of youth,
for the joys of parenthood
and the worries too.
Help those who are facing troubles
in relationships as well as finances,
in boundaries as well as freedom.
May growth and maturity
go hand in hand with aspiration and risk,
and may inspiration and creativity
never be stifled by conformity and safety first.
May we trust each other and you, Lord,
as we step forward in faith
and face the future together.
Amen.

Friend of family and family friend,
we ask for your blessings on all families,
those starting out on parenthood,
and those based on grandparents,
going forward and looking back.
May we cherish the memories of our upbringing,
and learn the lessons for our parenting.
Bring us:
joy and celebration;
comfort and support;
pride and passion;
honesty and truth;
openness and trust.
And may we learn all this from your Son,
our Saviour, Jesus Christ.
Amen.

Father of all,
look down on the human family,
with all our gifts and all our foibles,
and take a bow.
In your creation is every model –
and every warning – for our family life.
Help us to learn those lessons
and do our best to get things right.
And where we have been hurt
let us seek reconciliation, repentance and forgiveness.
Where we have been privileged
to experience or see real family love,
may that be a beacon for our lives,
a lantern for our feet.
And in all that is good
may we thank and praise you,
through your Son, Jesus Christ.
Amen.

God of compassion,
we pray for families broken apart
by conflict, pain and abuse.
May your healing hand be at work,
in mending human hearts
and giving hope in place of despair.
May all those supporting children and families
be blessed with caring instincts
be brave in professional assessments,
and be gifted with good insights,
as they seek to mediate rather than intervene,
give assistance rather than confront
but, above all, honour the example of your Son,
for whom every child matters
and who insists
that every child should be heard.
Amen.

# Birthdays

God of all ages,
pour your blessings on all those with birthdays this week:
thirty or ninety,
eight or eighty,
one or seventeen;
everyone is special in your eyes,
and may everyone with a birthday feel special too.
Give to all those around a reason to celebrate,
not just the day but the person,
not just the years but the gifting,
not just the milestone but the journey,
not just the past but the future.
May we gain perspective,
as we mark the years,
and count the blessings,
through your Son, our Saviour, Jesus Christ.
Amen.

Lord of all time,
we thank you for the celebration of birthdays,
for the celebration of life itself,
and for the person *(people)* celebrating a birthday today.
May *(name(s))* enjoy the day,
cherish the memories,
and look forward to what the future holds.
Renew in all of us a spirit of thankfulness,
knowing that the present is a gift
and an experience to be shared.
At the very time when people are focused on one person,
let it be a time for communal celebration
and another reason to thank you,
generous God.
Amen.

Heavenly Father,
as the angels rejoiced at the birth of your Son,
may every birthday bring joy,
every step along life's journey
bring new discoveries and new reasons to believe.
May your plan for us give us hope,
from day to day and year to year,
bringing us closer to you
but also closer to our inner selves,
when your Holy Spirit can bring us alive,
if we care to turn to you.
Make every birthday a time for renewal,
a time to be born again,
through the love of your Son, Jesus Christ.
Amen.

Dear God,
help us to celebrate this birthday as you would want,
in the lighting of candles
and blowing them out in one go;
in the sharing of cake
and handing it out to friends;
in the singing of silly songs
and not being embarrassed;
and in the giving and receiving of presents
and remembering to say 'thank you'.
Above all, let us have fun, Lord,
and commit our next year to do great things,
and walk in your way,
our Shepherd, Priest and King.
Amen.

# Graces

Lord,
this food and drink you give to us;
our praise and thanks we give to you.
Amen.

Almighty God,
bless this food
as we break this bread.
Bless this place
as we share our meal.
Bless us all
as we enjoy the fruits of your creation.
And before we eat and drink
we give thanks to you, Lord of all.
Amen.

Heavenly Father,
as we eat our food
may we sing your praise.
As we lift our glasses
may we offer you our thanks.
As we share our thoughts
may we think of our neighbour.
As we enjoy the plenty before us
may we remember the hungry around us,
as your Son asked us to do.
Amen.

Lord Almighty,
as we give you thanks for this meal,
may we show thanks in our lives.
Bless the food before us, we pray,
and all who helped to bring it to us today.
Amen.

Abundant God,
as you fill us up with good things,
make us grateful for the small things.
Open us up to your will and bring us all to your feast.
And as we eat together
may we never forget those who prepared this food,
those who cooked it
and those who do not have fair shares
of the abundance of your creation.
Amen.

Father of all,
thank you for feeding us;
thank you for needing us.
Bless those who serve
and those who conserve.
And let us be sharers as well as carers
as we enjoy this meal.
Amen.

Lord,
may this food do us good;
may this drink make us think!
And let us be grateful for this plateful.
Amen.

# Anniversaries

Lord of all time,
we give you thanks for this milestone.
May *(name)* and *(name)* look back with pride
and look forward with hope.
Let this day be a special day,
and may it be great for you too, Lord.
Help us to appreciate the commitment
two people have given to each other,
and may their relationship with you
be enfolded in love, inspire them in truth
and bring them at the last
to your eternal kingdom,
through Jesus Christ.
Amen.

God of partnership and promise,
create in us a commitment to each other
in marriage,
in civil partnership,
in family,
in friendship,
at work,
in church,
as neighbours,
in teams.
And may we celebrate significant anniversaries in all these areas,
especially today, as we remember
the anniversary of *(name)* and *(name)*.
Give us open minds and generous hearts,
as we join in the celebration.
Amen.

Gracious Lord,
you know and see things that really matter.
Today we ask for your blessing
on *(name)* and *(name)*
as they celebrate an important anniversary.
May their love be an example to others
and may their love for you
be stronger for their partnership.
Give to all your people
the capacity for self-giving love
through the example of your Son, Jesus Christ.
Amen.

Father, Son and Holy Spirit,
you have offered to us
a perfect sign of indivisibility,
a perfect partnership made in heaven,
but clearly evident here on earth.
May we take your example
in our long-term commitments to each other,
to our family,
to our church,
to our workplace,
to our charity of choice.
May trust develop from understanding,
sacrifice be offered through love,
and service be given without hesitation.
Bring us to a true appreciation
of what binds us together,
as you are bound together in trinity.
Amen.

# Death

God of beginnings and endings,
may our deaths be as memorable as our births,
if not for us, then for those around us.
May we not fear the inevitable,
but nor should we hasten it.
Help us to understand that both life and death
are miracles, are natural,
part of your greater scheme of things, Lord.
Give us the fortitude to understand this,
in ourselves as well as in others.
Help us to cope in the process of death,
for you have taken away its sting,
through the love of your Son, Jesus Christ.
Amen.

Eternal God,
your Son has showed us that sin and death can be conquered.
Strengthen us in our understanding of this last frontier,
so that our minds can comprehend what our hearts tell us:
that beyond the veil lies your peace;
that we will meet our parents and forebears once more;
that we will no longer feel any suffering;
and that we will bask in your closer presence,
all in the knowledge and certainty that your Son taught us.
Amen.

God of time and place,
may our time here on earth be worthy of you;
and may our legacy be that your creation is not tainted.
We thank you for the life of *(name)* as we say farewell.
Our memories are rich;
our hearts are full;
our loss is great;
and our tears flow.
Let us all take inspiration
from a life well lived,
a family founded on love
and a lasting influence on us all.
We thank you, Lord, and ask for the peace
that only you can give.
Amen.

Glorious God,
may the death of *(name)* cause us to step back,
remembering a full life,
grieving a lost life,
hoping for the peace of eternal life.
We pray for those who mourn, including ourselves.
We pray for those who have cared and supported.
We pray for the communities which have lost a member.
And we pray for the friend we had,
who is now in your closer presence
and whom we will see again,
if we are granted a place in your eternal kingdom,
loving Lord.
Amen.

# Remembrance

Almighty God,
we give thanks for the sacrifice
of those who gave their lives in war.
We remember especially the allied forces
in two world wars,
as well as those who fell in more recent conflicts,
including the Falklands, Iraq and Afghanistan.
In a moment of silence we remember individuals
among our friends *(pause for silence),*
among our families *(pause for silence),*
from our community *(pause for silence).*
We salute the bravery that took them far from home
and acknowledge the grief of loved ones back home.
May we always remember;
may we never forget.
Amen.

God of remembrance,
no one is forgotten in your eyes,
whether they are here on earth
or with you in heaven:
the youngest, the oldest;
the courageous, the timid;
the single person, the family member;
the able, the disabled.
All have played their part in your world
and have a place in your kingdom,
through your grace and their faith.
May we long remember all who went before,
especially those whose lives were cut short through war
and whose efforts have made the rest of us safer.
We ask this through the one who sacrificed all for us,
Jesus Christ, our Saviour.
Amen

Lord of life and death,
give us the hope that your Son brought,
even when it is hard to bear the loss of loved ones.
Give us the promise of eternity for those we see no more.
Give to those who mourn fond memories of life in its abundance.
Create in us all the capacity to be truly grateful
to those who went before;
to those who fought and died for our freedom;
to those who care for injured service personnel
and to those who remain to guard us now, Lord.
We ask this through our Saviour, Jesus Christ.
Amen.

God of power and mercy,
we ask for your blessings on our service personnel
in two world wars;
in countless conflicts around the world;
in defence of the realm;
in peacekeeping missions;
in support of democracy.
At this time we remember
those who gave their lives to keep us safe;
those who were injured in the line of duty;
the loved ones of the dead and maimed
over the years, including today.
We ask especially that those we remember
are at peace in your eternal kingdom
and are remembered not just once a year
but in our hearts and minds throughout the year.
Amen.

# Thanksgiving

Almighty God,
may we always show our thanks to you
in the way we live,
in the way we hope,
in the way we pray,
in the way we praise your name.
It is a blessing that we can worship you
and a duty too, as
'All things come from you
and of your own do we give you.'
Bring us to a true appreciation
of your creation in all its richness,
so that we can live life abundantly,
as your Son taught us.
Amen.

Bountiful Lord,
help us to express our thanks,
genuinely and generously,
when by your grace we know your joy.
We know we cannot earn your love,
nor can we assume we deserve it.
But we thank you, gracious God,
that you revealed your love for us
through sending your Son to live among us,
by sending your Holy Spirit to dwell within us
and to give us a glimpse of your glory,
through the death, resurrection and ascension of your Son,
Our Saviour, Jesus Christ.
Amen.

Heavenly Father,
grant us the capacity to see the generosity of your creation.
Give us the insight to see your vision for humankind.
We thank you for showing us your leading light,
a light to the world,
a lamp for our feet,
a laser to your love.
With you we have no limitations to our aspirations.
Without you we will fall short of our potential.
Create in us true thanksgiving
and the desire to do much more for you
in honour of the gifts you continue to shower on us,
through your Son, our Saviour, Jesus Christ.
Amen.

God of gifting,
renew in us the intention to understand
and the capacity to wonder.
May we give thanks where thanks are due:
to parents, who love and nurture us;
to family, who protect and stand up for us;
to schools, for stretching our minds;
to each other for our relationships;
but above all, Lord,
to the one who died for us
and who has never turned his back on us,
your Son, our Saviour, Jesus Christ.
Amen.

# Festivals, seasons and saints

# Advent

God of light and might,
bring to our world a new beginning,
a fresh start for your people.
We give thanks for the anticipation
of promises fulfilled that John heralded.
May we rejoice in all that lies ahead
as we move from darkness to light,
from repentance to forgiveness,
from despair to hope.
Help us to be prepared for change,
in ourselves and in your Church,
for now and for ever.
Amen.

God of hope,
at this time we look forward in anticipation
and look back in thankfulness.
Bless all those who pave the way for others,
remembering especially the ministry of John the Baptist.
As we await the coming of the Light of the World,
may we reach out to others
and bring them into the light,
out of the shadow of darkness.
Renew and restore us,
so that we can play our part
in your great mission to the world,
through your Son, Jesus Christ.
Amen.

Loving Lord,
as we embark on the season of Advent,
help us to take stock of our faith
and to prepare the way on our own journey.
We give thanks for the promise of forgiveness,
through John's ministry of repentance through baptism,
and eagerly await the restoration of our relationship with you
through the coming of your Son at Bethlehem.
As Mary and Joseph patiently waited,
so may we be faithful and watchful
in our prayers and penitence.
Amen.

Almighty God,
create in us this Advent
a sense of your presence;
a knowledge of your love;
a certainty of your hope;
and an understanding of your promise.
Shine a light in our lives
to expose our failings;
to highlight our penitence;
to renew our faith;
and to prepare us for the coming of your Son,
as John the Baptist did.
Amen.

# Christmas

God of new beginnings,
we rejoice with the angels
at the birth of your Son.
May we share the gift of hope
that this day brings for humankind.
Give us focus and friendship
so that real peace, your peace,
can break out – and be sustained.
As we watch and shepherds gather,
may the star of Bethlehem
shine brightly in our lives.
Amen.

Almighty God,
we ask for your blessings
and offer you our thanks,
as Christmas once again enters our lives and hearts.
May the birth of your Son
bring gladness and neighbourliness,
even where there is hardship and suffering.
May our actions and thoughts
reflect the generosity of the gift of your Son, Jesus Christ,
to a world in need of your love.
Amen.

Loving and faithful God,
you have entrusted your Son
to a world that rejected you,
giving humankind a second chance.
At this festive season, help us to seize the time
to give a second chance
to family relationships;
to help for neighbours;
to global awareness;
and above all, Lord,
to our relationship with you,
through our Emmanuel,
born this day.
Amen.

God of hope,
lead us to your Son
as we remember his birth.
Lead us to better ways
as we follow his ways.
Lead us to watch and worship
as the shepherds show us.
Lead us to celebrate in song
as we join the music of the angels.
May the lasting legacy of that first Christmas
be that we put you first,
not just once a year, but for all time,
as your Son did.
Amen.

# Epiphany

Lord of signs and symbols,
as the star beckoned magi from distant lands,
so are we drawn by the birth of your Son,
over time as well as space.
Help us in our own age to go the extra mile,
to learn your ways and witness to your truth.
As we gather round the crib,
in church or in our imagination,
may we feel the anticipation of all around,
the humble and mighty,
brought together in wonder,
held together with hope,
as we are today.
Amen.

Gracious God,
the gift of your Son was heralded by angels
and marked by the star that drew the magi.
But we thank you that it was the shepherds
who were the first witnesses and the early evangelists,
as the word was spread about the holy birth.
Give us the vision to be there now,
in the outhouse among the animals,
Mary with the child and Joseph standing by.
As our Christmas gifts lose their shine,
may your gift to us grow in importance,
shaping our lives and pointing us to a bright future with you,
ever-loving Lord.
Amen.

Great Shepherd of the sheep,
the birth of your Son changed everything
and changes us still.
May we carry forward into the new year
our hopes and your expectations,
the goodwill of Christmas,
the mended relationships
and the spirit of giving and receiving.
But help us also, Lord,
to forgive any harsh words,
to get over disappointments
and to renew the spirit of love,
in response to the great gift
of your Son, our Saviour, Jesus Christ.
Amen.

God of all ages and all time,
create in us the wonder felt by the magi
as they travelled far in faith and hope.
Send your Holy Spirit to awaken in us
the surprise of the shepherds,
the acceptance of Joseph,
the joy of the angels,
the love of Mary,
and the realisation that all things are made new
in our relationship with you
and in the tender mercy of your grace,
which oversees your creation
and fills our lives
if we are open to your love.
Amen.

# Lent

Forgiving Lord,
may our Lenten journey bring us close to you
as we discipline ourselves
in study and in our daily lives,
taking new things on if we give things up
and opening our minds to new insights along the way.
Send us out in persistence and faith
to demonstrate the care and concern
your Son showed us in his life and death.
It is the least that we can do
to show our gratitude
to the one who saved us
and suffered for us,
your Son, Jesus Christ.
Amen.

Heavenly Father,
at this time we offer you our persistence and praise
through fasting and giving up,
but also through studying and taking on.
May what we learn renew our hope
and bring us closer to your purpose.
As we seek to follow your Son's example,
in prayer, in social action, in selfless love,
give us strength to withstand the pressures of society,
which can draw us away,
as our discipline slips
and our faith falters.
Empower us with your Spirit,
equip us in your service.
Amen.

Almighty God,
bring to us new insights this Lent,
so that in our worship and daily practice
we grow closer to you.
Let us for once put aside selfishness
and let your Son's selflessness draw us to him.
In learning what we miss
may we learn what we really need
but also what is required by others around:
neighbours, friends, and families,
as well as our neighbours across the world,
part of your family of humankind,
all made in your image.
Grant us the gift of peace
in the midst of the world's busyness.
Amen.

Lord God,
may we be tested in the wilderness
as your Son was.
May we find ourselves alone with you
as your Son was.
May we learn to be connected with you
as your Son was.
But, in this Lenten period
as we approach the events of Holy Week,
let us give thanks that we are spared
the consequences of our past sins
through the forgiveness and salvation
taught and acted out
in your Son's ministry and suffering,
leading to the sacrifice of the crucifixion
and his glorious resurrection.
For all this, we thank and glorify you,
gracious God.
Amen.

# Easter

God of glory,
we sing your praises this special day.
Halleluiah, risen Lord!
Halleluiah, love triumphant!
Halleluiah, Redeemer, Saviour!
May the joy that we feel
create a wave of peace and celebration
which washes away doubt and fear
and brings hope and reconciliation
to a broken world
and a new beginning for humankind.
Amen.

Father of all,
we give thanks that your promise has been fulfilled,
that your Son has broken through the barrier of death
for us and for all humankind,
having taken on the burden of our sins:
all have been washed away in the blood of Good Friday
and now the transformation is accomplished
through the resurrection of that first Easter morning.
May prophet and priest, president and monarch,
rejoice with us and all the saints,
that we are held in your hands,
shielded and redeemed by your Son,
our Saviour, Jesus Christ.
Amen.

God of promise and purpose,
we thank you that your Son
risked all for us, in his life and death.
We rejoice with you at his rising to new life,
such as you promised for those
who keep firm in faith and true to you.
May we seek to extend your kingdom
in every way we can,
in church and in community,
in witness and in mission,
so that the good news continues
from generation to generation
and extends to every neighbourhood,
near and far, accessible and remote.
Inspire us daily as we have been inspired today.
Alleluiah, alleluiah.
Amen.

Heavenly Father,
say it's so,
that Christ is risen.
Make it so,
that we are saved.
Let it be,
that you are with us.
Help us see
that death is conquered.
As we start afresh, in hope and trust,
lead us by the example of your Son
and the guidance of your Holy Spirit,
so that we can accomplish
all that your risen Son would wish.
Amen.

# Ascension

Faithful God,
at this Ascensiontide we give thanks
for entrusting us with your Son,
for never giving up on us,
even though we have often ignored you.
As your Son ascends and your Spirit descends,
we ask for your blessings on our Church,
which you have empowered and equipped
to sustain the faith,
to nurture disciples,
and to continue the task
begun, inspired and continued
through the risen Christ.
Amen.

Blessed Trinity,
reunited and indivisible,
strengthen us in our daily round,
our common tasks, our mission duties.
In church and in prayer,
restore and renew our trust in you,
so that we can extend your kingdom
in the sure knowledge of your love and oversight.
You have transformed us through the cross,
trusted us in the Ascension,
equipped as through the Spirit.
Accompany us in our journey
as we explore our path back to you,
safe at last.
Amen.

Loving Lord,
let us always give thanks for gifts
that help us to grow in faith.
Just as you sent your Son
on a mercy mission to save fallen humankind,
so your Son put in place a stairway to heaven
through the perseverance of your disciples
in building up your Church
so that where your Son has gone
we may follow.
By your grace and our faith
may we join him on that stairway,
through your Son, Jesus Christ.
Amen.

Eternal Father,
your Son restored, redeemed and brought us back to you.
As he ascends to your right hand,
we rejoice at the scale of his intervention,
at the sheer transforming power of his love
and your great goodness in sending him to us.
We are no longer on our own,
as we have the Holy Spirit, the Comforter,
to guide our path and order our ways.
May we be faithful and fruitful
in discharging our duties through your Church,
dear Lord and father of humankind.
Amen.

# Pentecost

Almighty God,
fill us with your Holy Spirit,
such as your disciples experienced
in the rush of wind at Pentecost,
enabling, empowering, enthusing,
giving fresh insights and new understanding.
May we call on your Spirit
in good times and bad,
in sleep and rest,
and may we share with confidence
our faith, our hope, your truth.
Breathe on me, breath of God
and set my spirit free.
Amen.

Transforming God,
bring us the gift of communication,
just as you set the disciples free
to speak in different tongues
and be understood by all.
May we always seek to engage with people
in ways and in language
both appropriate and sensitive.
Never let us withhold understanding of your word,
through teaching, metaphor or example
that fails to be true to you
and falls short of the clarity
your Son would wish.
Amen.

God of our Church,
let us welcome the breath of fresh air of your Holy Spirit,
in our worship,
in our hearts,
in our relationships,
in our parish life.
May the flames of faith be fanned
as we listen eagerly to your word.
And may we be touched
by the love you have shown
in sending the Holy Spirit as Comforter,
through Jesus Christ, our Lord.
Amen.

God of hope and help,
we are doubly blessed
through the coming of the Holy Spirit
to guide us on the path your Son showed us.
May we, in church and at home,
be constantly refreshed and truly transformed
when we turn to you,
not just for ourselves
but for friends and family
and for people across the world,
so that we can be better instruments of your peace
and good communicators, in word and deed,
of your kingdom.
Amen.

# Saints

Holy Lord,
as we celebrate St *(name)*
we remember all the saints,
those who are special to us and our church,
those whose stories still inspire us today,
those unnamed saints whose unsung witness made a difference
and those who are the saints of today, in your eyes, Lord.
Allow us our human role models,
who followed the example of your Son,
some even to death.
We thank you for their lives and their story, Lord.
Amen.

Loving Lord,
in remembering our patron, St *(name)*
we honour *her* name and give thanks for *her* life.
May we learn from the witness and sacrifice of all the saints,
be inspired by their faithfulness
and share their stories with others.
Give us the confidence which they had
to proclaim your name and keep your laws.
In a moment's silence, we bring before you
the saints of today who serve you
in ways which advance your kingdom *(silence).*
Lord, uphold them in their mission.
Amen.

Generous God,
you have poured your gifts on the saints through the ages.
Bring learning and purpose to our study of saints, day by day.
In this place, on this day, we give thanks for St *(name).*
May our lives be shaped by the legacy of this and all the saints,
not in place of that of your Son,
but to illuminate the path he trod,
the way, the truth, and the life he revealed
and the redemption he bought us,
in the lives of saints and martyrs.
Amen.

Eternal God,
as we celebrate the saints in heaven
and the saints of the Christian Church,
so we acknowledge the sainthood of all believers.
May all those who profess your name
be mindful of the saints who have gone before.
And in a moment's silence
we recall those saints who have special meaning for us
*(silence).*
May we grow to be more like them
in our faith, our life, our hope.
Amen.

# Arrow prayers

Lord, hear our intercessions as we listen to your word.

Let us know the mind of Christ
as well as feel his love.

Make us whole
in body and soul.

Give me hope in the darkness, Lord,
and consolation in my sorrow.

May our joy never be at another's expense.

May our sorrows be shared
by friends who care, including your Son.

Immanent God, always on hand,
guide me all the days of my life.

Lord, help me to hope, teach me to trust.

Above all, Lord, may I see you more clearly, day by day.

Bring me sleep to refresh my body.
Bring me peace to refresh my soul.

Let it be you, Lord, to grant me your peace.
Let it be me, Lord, to give you my heart.

Send me out to preach your word and save a soul.

May I survive the test and give you my best.

Lord, with you there is no mission impossible.

Let me go along your way, not mine.

Keep me from harm, keep others safe.

Lord, may our journey bring great expectation
and our arrival great joy.

Watch over me as I grow spiritually.
Top up my energy and refresh my search for truth.

Bring me sun to cheer me.
Send me rain to cool me.

Guide my footsteps please, Lord,
both uphill and downhill.
Let healing do its work
and wholeness be the outcome,
by your grace, not my faith.

As nature provides, your love guides.

May this church flourish, if it is your wish.

God of purpose, show us your will.
God of mission, send us out to serve.

Lord, bring me hope at the start
and even more hope at the end.

# Resources for praying

**Personal: preparing your own**

If anyone can say a prayer then anyone can write a prayer. There really is no mystique about it; only authenticity is needed if the prayer is to encapsulate your own thoughts, praise, supplication and intercession. I have found that, if you want to write a prayer, let your mind and heart have their way and just write – or type. You can always amend the wording or 'top and tail' the prayer afterwards. That's why extemporary prayer can be so powerful, as people say what is in their heart. However, the beauty of composition on paper is that there is a natural editing process, which should ensure that some of the dangers of extemporary prayer, its repetitions and additions, are avoided. So try it, perhaps as a result of finding that the right prayer for you is not in this book after all!

You might want to prepare your own prayers specifically for use in your church, referring to the name of your church as you pray, or you could write prayers for people to use when they pop into church and need just one or two to aid them in their meditations. (Examples of each type are set out on the following pages.) These could be made available for use in church either on card for reuse (or for sale) or simply on sheets which could be taken away and used at home.

For church (prepared for my church, Holy Trinity in Folkestone):

Lord God,
Father, Son and Holy Spirit,
watch over our church and our people.
Let peace and love fill our church life.
Let worship and music fill this sacred space.
Let prayer and contemplation
fill our hearts and minds.
Give to this church the sense of your immanence
and a glimpse of your purpose,
so that our church is your Church
and our people your people.
Amen.

Almighty God,
three in one and one in three,
send down upon us the fruits of your Spirit,
so that our mission can be yours
and our aims can be true.
May the Holy Trinity be evident in this place,
in our worship and our praise.
And may the beauty of our building
inspire our actions in the world,
attracting visitors and pilgrims on their journeys
to experience your love,
through Father, Son and Holy Spirit.
Amen.

Heavenly Father,
we give you thanks for the vision
of those who built this church.
May your Spirit breathe life into our worship.
May your Son inspire us through your word.
May your grace and forgiveness fill our lives.
Bless this place and our purpose
and make us worthy, as a church and congregation,
to honour you in name and follow you in prayer.
Amen.

For personal use:

**A prayer for peace**

Lord God,
I pray for your peace in a broken world
and for your hope in a restless world.
Grant me calm when I am tense
and reflection when I am under pressure.
May your Church, this church,
help me to focus my thoughts on your will for me
and bring me the perfect peace
that your Son has promised, now and for ever.
Amen.

**A prayer for loved ones**

Heavenly Father,
keep safe all those I love
and especially at this time *(names).*
Give comfort and healing to those who are unwell,
remembering in particular *(names).*
May they know your love
and feel your presence in their lives.
Grant those who are now at peace with you
the joy of eternal life
and the blessings of your closer presence,
leaving us with fond memories.
Amen.

**A prayer for oneself**

God of love and grace,
watch over me as I stumble.
Be with me as I pick myself up.
Guide me in my faith journey
and bring me safe home at the last.
I ask this through the one who knows me best
and who will give me rest,
your Son, our Saviour, Jesus Christ.
Amen.

**Books and other sources**

The sources of prayers old and new are amazing. Not only do we have the legacy of prayers from centuries gone by which are still treasure troves of distilled wisdom and holiness, but we also have the internet to draw on and, lest we forget, the glories of the *Common Worship* book of services and prayers for the Church of England, from the General Thanksgiving (if in doubt, use this!) to the Collects; or the majesty of the prayers from the Book of Common Prayer, or the modern Litany. Most leading publishers have a great variety of books of prayers, both compilations and original compositions. But dusty bookshops, church vestry shelves and charity shops can offer gems that are well worth seeking out. And please support your local Christian bookshop if you have one – or the nearest Christian conference or retreat centre.

**Retreats and parish days of prayer**

Many churches have parish away-days, retreats or quiet days. Prayer is usually – and should be – at the heart of these. It is probably worth giving proper thought and preparation time to the role of prayer, rather than leaving things solely to the Holy Spirit on the day! Find a theme or a book to use as a basis for your prayer time or ask each member to bring a prayer that means a lot personally, but is relevant to the theme chosen or the main issues being addressed. Remember that prayer is all about active engagement, including active listening, so a framework and a purpose are helpful, for those steeped in prayer and those unused to extended prayer alike. And if in our churches there are regular 'Songs of Praise' services, with hymns and songs chosen by the congregation, why not a 'Prayers of Praise' service, with favourite prayers chosen in the same way, with all the opportunities for testimony that could bring?